Reflections Beneath the Buckeye Trees

Reflections Beneath the Buckeye Trees

For

Joseph Spinoza Elkins

Uncle Spi

"Your granddaddy would sure get a kick out of you."

For

Jess Lee Fisher Sr.

Uncle Jess

"Now, go get'em.

Copyright © 2026 Antwone Fisher

All rights reserved.

No part of this book may be reproduced or transmitted in any form or by any means,

electronic or mechanical, including photocopying, recording, or by any information

storage and retrieval system, without prior written permission from the publisher.

Published by Glenville House Press

Printed in the United States of America

Glenville House Press
Cleveland, Ohio

Contents

Glenville 1

Light on the Wall 7

The Drawing 11

The Man in the Graveyard 13

My Mother 21

The Dream That Held Me 29

Down in Mississippi 33

The Day I Got Humbled 43

My Social Workers 47

Mercy 51

Valencia 59

The 4th of July 63

The Voice Before the Sermon 67

Did You Read About Me? 73

Mr. Nobody 77

Way to Come Back Home! 83

CSU 89

Pamela Louis 91

The Kiss 95

The Day I Married LaNette 99

Once You're a Father 103

I Fell in Love with Words 109

Tyrone 113

Hong Kong	117
Getting Out	121
Todd	123
Enem	129
Denzel	133
The Sandman	139
The Coat and the Chicken	143
Antwone Days	147
A Faithful Warner	149
Endure	151
Restoring the Color	155
Skipping Across the Years	159
Black Sand	163
So Many Stars	167
Sasebo	169
School Boy Crush	173
What You See Is What You Get	179
The Boy Inside the Man	185
Janise Womick	189
The Homecoming	197
Where Were You?!	203
Misunderstood	207
The Hidden People	211
Our Souls Are Tired	217
Who I Am	227

What Forgiveness Gave Me	233
My Shyness	245
What Time Doesn't Take	249
From the Outside Looking In	251
Proof of Life	255
Afterword	261
Acknowledgments	263
About the Author	267
Also by Antwone Fisher	269

Foreword

I believe we're living through the middle of the end of everything we once knew America to be—and that could mean different things to different people. For some, it may signal total collapse. For others, it could be a long-awaited shift—joy coming in the morning, a chariot swinging low to carry us home.

And maybe now—before more slips away—it's time to look back. To sift through our lives and hold onto even the smallest, most personal moments that shaped us. Because that's where the meaning lives. In what we've seen. What we've survived. And what, if anything, we've learned.

I've lived a life I couldn't have imagined as a boy—from being born in prison to having lunch with a president's family in the private quarters of the White House. I've stood in rooms I never thought I'd see.

But the most important lessons, the ones that truly formed me, didn't come from fame or success. They came from the streets I walked, the people I loved, and the quiet moments that often go unnoticed. Those are the reflections I'm sharing in these pages.

This book isn't a timeline. It's not arranged by date or even by chapter. It's a gathering of memory—of truth as I lived it. Some of these pieces are tender. Some are raw. Some are full of joy, and others are heavy with the kind of silence that stays with you for years. But all of them come from a place I carry with me every day.

And so, I begin where I began.

Glenville.

Introduction

Antwone Fisher is an unusual man, I know no other way to put it. He is a curious man, open-minded, willing to look again rather than give an experience the once over.
It has been my pleasure and privilege to visit with Mr. Fisher on a weekly basis, to hear his take on a variety of matters, to laugh together having tickled each other's fancy. Sometimes he wipes away tears of laughter; at other times, he suddenly becomes seized by an eruption of deep grief. His emotions run the gamut; he is very much "in touch" with himself, more than most.
Mr. Fisher has seen a lot and he has been through a lot, and while such harrowing experiences might fell a lesser man, they only served to strengthen him. He survived the foster care system, which deposited him unceremoniously onto the streets at so young an age one wonders how he managed to avoid getting locked up, as so many men in his shoes tend to do. Mr. Fisher is the embodiment of resilience.
What is most remarkable is his unassuming nature, his uncanny calm, and his surprisingly powerful powers of observation. I have rarely met a more literate man; his mind is a marvel. He can step back, far enough back, to see what else there might be to see—sights and smells that escape the notice of others. Smells anchor many of his

favored memories; smells he brings to life; smells I too can smell by the magical act of his describing them to me. Mr. Fisher's ability to put his experiences into words is nothing short of poetic. Read what he has written, and I think you will agree. I am forever wowed by his level of wonder, what he can and does teach me from his days at sea, from his days working as a guard at the penitentiary. I could go on and on about this remarkable man, but that would distract you from diving in and experiencing him for yourself. Enjoy.

—Richard Tuch, MD

Author's Note

I've lived long enough to know that survival is only the beginning.
What you do with the days after—that's the true measure.
These pages are not an account of victories or wounds.
They are proof of life, carried forward in fragments, moments, and memories that refused to be lost.
I wrote them to remind myself that even in the hardest seasons, there was always something worth holding on to—a sound, a kindness, a glimmer of light. And I wrote them for those who may need that reminder too.
If you find yourself in these reflections, know this: you are not alone. The past can break you, but it can also shape you. And if you let it, it can even raise you up.
This book is my offering. Not as an ending, but as evidence that a life—no matter how hidden or battered—holds meaning.
And that meaning is worth speaking into the world.
Excelsior.

—Antwone Fisher

This book is meant to be lingered with, not hurried through.

Each reflection is a doorway—to a street, a memory, a moment when time seemed to hold still.

Read them slowly. Let the words breathe. Let the sound of Lake Erie's roar, the scent of summer leaves, and the hush of a boyhood street find you where you are.

These pages are not just about what happened, but about what remains—
the voice that rose from it all.

Glenville

I grew up in Glenville, once its own little east-side village, just a short walk from the roaring expanse of Lake Erie, before the city of Cleveland, Ohio, claimed it. Over time, Glenville changed. It grew into a lively Black community, cradled beneath a canopy of trees so lush and green they seemed to hold the world still, softening the edges of time. If Cleveland was my home, then Glenville was my bedroom—the place where I slept, dreamed, and became myself. My world was bordered by Superior Avenue, East 105th Street, DuPont Avenue, and Parkwood Drive. Inside those lines was everything I knew. Everything that knew me.

It was the late 1960s and early 1970s, and though signs of segregation no longer appeared on fountains and doors, you could still feel it. Redlining, scarce jobs, and quiet city policies guided Black families into certain corners of town—not by force, but by design. And that design shaped everything.

The houses—including the one where I grew up on Drexel—were a hundred years old or more, grand Victorian homes with wide front porches, creaking staircases, and basements anchored by heavy furnaces. They stood beneath trees that lined the streets like elders, shoulder to shoulder under the green watch of willows, maples, oaks, and sycamores—and, of course, Buckeye trees.

Cleveland, Ohio, had a few nicknames back then—the Plum City, the Forest City— and in Glenville, Forest City made perfect sense. In autumn, leaves tumbled through the air like confetti, filling the streets with a potpourri of earth, memory, and color. We were just a couple of miles from mighty Lake Erie, and on certain days, if the wind was right, you could catch its scent. Sometimes a fog would roll across the water from Canada and settle in our streets like a soft blanket, making the neighborhood feel even more tucked away—almost dreamlike.

Summers were hot and muggy. There was no air conditioning, so people sat on their porches late into the night, cooling themselves with their church fans—the kind with Dr. King's face on one side and a funeral home ad on the back. Radios hummed softly with soul music from the local Black stations—WJMO or WABQ. Fireflies floated through the thick air, blinking like stars that had drifted down to our block. I'd walk to the corner store for a popsicle, passing open doors, screen doors, folks calling out to one another. It felt like the whole neighborhood was alive, exhaling together in the heat.

Glenville had parks—real parks—with swings, polished heavy metal sliding boards, and merry-go-rounds nested between the blocks, always alive with children after school and on weekends, their voices rising in that unmistakable music only childhood can make.

We didn't have toys, not like today. We used our imaginations. We played red-light-green-light, Mother May I, jumped rope, shot marbles, played jacks. It was safe. Folks looked out for one another's children. And friendships were made—some that lasted a lifetime.

We all knew when to head home. When the streetlights came on, that was the signal. No one had to tell us. Looking back, I realize Glenville gave me something rare— a kind of peace. A pocket of protection. I knew about racism and prejudice, but I didn't feel it pressing down on me in my day-to-day. In some strange way, segregation shielded me from the full brunt of it, even as it limited our world.

Our neighborhood held every walk of life—Black preachers, policemen, firemen, electricians, barbers, business owners. Some folks were wealthy, with well-kept homes and shiny cars. Others rented small apartments or got by week to week. But the beauty of it was—they all lived side by side. The well-off became a kind of quiet governor, setting a tone of dignity and steadiness that echoed through the community. Even those who lived in the shadows—the hustlers, the underworld folks—kept things in check. Crime existed, but there was still a sense of order, of balance. A hum of decency that held the neighborhood together.

And in that spirit, money wasn't always what mattered. I remember my foster mother paying the local barber for our haircuts with a soul food lunch plate—collard greens, cornbread, black-eyed peas and rice, and yes, a couple pieces of perfectly seasoned fried chicken from last night's supper.

By the mid-1970s, things began to come apart. As housing anti-discrimination laws were enforced more seriously, families with means moved into other parts of the city. Desegregation meant Glenville's children were bused out of the neighborhood—and with them went the clamor and laughter from our playgrounds. The bonds between children quietly frayed. Too many lost touch.

The Glenville I had known—that little east-side village I first saw through my young eyes—began to fade. The balance we'd lived with slipped away. Those who remained were often the ones with fewer options, and the community's safety net thinned. That beautiful, storybook place—full of fireflies, soul music, and corner grocers who'd give you credit when you were short—began to disappear.

But I lived in that golden time. I knew that Glenville. It was my bedroom in the great house of Cleveland—the place where I learned how to dream, how to endure, how to become. And when I look back on it now, it's like gazing into a Norman Rockwell painting—only this one is painted in Black, with deeper tones and fuller truths.

And it was beautiful.

Light on the Wall

When I was a little boy, I slept in a narrow, heavy iron cot —just wide enough to hold me.
The headboard and footboard folded flat for easy storage. Every sunny morning, sunlight found its way in and bathed the room in a soft glow.

One morning, I noticed a single streak of light spilling across the wall beside my bed—golden and warm—like it was saying "good morning" the moment I opened my eyes.
I turned to look at the window and admired how it lit up the powder-blue curtains and cast that pretty glow across the room.
When I turned back to the wall, I realized the streak of sunlight had moved—spreading wider across the wall.

I made it a game to catch the light in the act of slipping.
It felt like the sun was playing with me, offering a little show.

That fascination kept hold of me from about age three to five.
But around six, something began to fade.
Not because my childhood was over—

but a new awareness began to distract me from everything I once found wondrous in the world.

The light still came.

But I had stopped looking for it.

And maybe the sun felt that too. Maybe it noticed when it lost me.

Because not long after, the sunlight changed.

Now it came through beveled glass in the living room—refracted, glowing with jewel tones and soft pastels.

It would scatter across the wall or glide across the room like something alive.

And in my head, I heard it say,

"Hey, Antwone... check this out."

It would stop me in my tracks.

Sometimes it gave me a chill, the way jewel tones sometimes do.

Other times, I felt like I was the only one who noticed it.

I wondered why no one else ever brought it up—which made me keep quiet about it.

Maybe it was just for me, I thought—chasing its quiet footsteps across the wall or standing in awe of its colors, appearing out of nowhere and dancing through my little world like magic.

Years later, at summer camp, I found myself hiking with other campers through dense woods—and once again, every ray of sun that broke through the treetops felt like it was meant for me.

The wind moved the branches, and the trees swayed as if conducting an unseen orchestra.

The leaves rustled overhead, adding their own sound—a soft applause—as shafts of sunlight burst through, turning the forest into a spectacular daytime light show. Flashes of gold and white danced over the green leaves, ran across the bark of the trunks, and spilled like glitter across the forest floor.

Ever the winsome boy, I felt my head spin—dizzy with the beauty of it all—while the other boys in the group didn't even seem to notice.

So I decided it must be just for me.

I let myself have it—
all of it—

while no one else even noticed.

The Drawing

As a boy, social services sent me to see a child psychiatrist.
He asked me to draw a picture.
And so I did.
 I drew a man who had fallen from a building.
The ground cracked beneath him.
But the man was unharmed.
 The psychiatrist's report said I had a fear of bodily harm.
Maybe that was true.
But what no one knew then—not him, not me—was the story still forming in the silence.
 Because two months before I was born,
my father was murdered.
Shot by a woman he had two children with.
A blast from a shotgun that almost severed him in two.
 I never knew him.
I was still in the womb.
But... I remembered.
Somehow, I drew it.
 Not the exact moment. Not the blood.
But the fall. The crack. The impact.
And a strange, silent survival.

Maybe the man I drew was my father.
Maybe it was me. Maybe it was both of us—tangled in a truth passed down through blood and sorrow.

This wasn't imagination.
It was ancestral memory.
It was the soul trying to explain what the world hadn't yet told me.

Even as a child, I was trying to say:
"Something broke before I arrived. But I'm still here."

And now I know.
The drawing wasn't a warning.
It was a witness.

And I've carried it ever since.

The Man in the Graveyard

When I was a boy, I didn't know the people I lived with weren't my real parents—not until my foster sister Valencia told me. We had just been punished again. The house was quiet and heavy, and we sat cross-legged and teary-eyed, as if waiting for something longed for but never to come. Then Valencia turned to me and Dwight and said, with attitude and defiance, "She ain't our real mother anyway."

I looked at her and asked, "Well, who is?"

She said, "I don't know who your mother is. But me and Dwight have the same mother."

When our foster mother found out Valencia had told us, she berated her for years. I never understood why—she reminded us often enough in her "don't nobody want you" rants. Still, that was when the questions began: Who was my mother? Who was my father?

I always had dreams. Some comforted me. Some scared me. Some turned into full-blown nightmares. But they were always there—like another room I could slip into when the real world got too heavy.

After that day, I started having dreams of the graveyard. I didn't say anything out loud. I just carried the questions with me. In one of those dreams, there was a young Black man. He never spoke. He never got close. He would just walk through the graveyard—sometimes looking at me, sometimes away. I watched him. He looked cool, I thought. Maybe this is my father. It was just a feeling. A quiet knowing.

I used to watch a scary show called *Dark Shadows*, and the graveyard in my dream looked just like the one on TV—foggy, dim, with fake headstones. I thought everyone had dreams like that, but some of mine never left me: the one I wrote about in *Finding Fish*, and the one that opens the *Antwone Fisher* film—where my ancestors meet me at a dining table.

Over time, I began to understand that some dreams aren't just dreams. They're something more. And I never forgot the ones that seemed to mean something.

When I was fourteen, my foster mother told me to go back where I came from. I was removed from the foster home and placed in the Mesenbaum Children's Center.

That was the start of my odyssey—through reform school, homelessness and the Navy. And through it all, I thought about my father.

The day I was removed, my social worker, Ms. Neese, sat me down, opened my file, and told me my father's name: Edward. It was the first time I'd heard it. It felt like a tentacle burst out of my heart and latched onto that name.

She showed me a newspaper article from the *Call & Post*. It said he'd been murdered. She read parts aloud, then paused, pointed to a line, and said, "He was killed in June. You were born that August." Then she added my mother had been incarcerated at the time—locked up in a girls' institution when I was born.

And I want to be clear: my mother had nothing to do with my father's murder. Some people have misunderstood. But the truth is, my father was murdered by someone else entirely—not by my mother.

Years later, after I'd left the Navy, I decided to search for him—for his family. I called the *Call & Post*, but they didn't keep old articles. They referred me to the Cleveland Public Library, where someone found the article on microfiche and mailed it to me.

When I opened the envelope and read it, the words felt like a punch:

"The victim Edward Elkins, 23, of 975 Parkwood Drive, was literally blasted down the stairs from the second-floor chain-locked door of Frances Holden, 19."

Thursday, June 4, 1959. Eighty-one degrees, warm and dry—an ordinary day on East 90th in Glenville, until Eddie was killed. Neighbors filled the sidewalks as word raced through porches, corner stores, churches, and the *Call & Post*.

I could see the rest—the part the article wouldn't say.

The shotgun blast tore through him with such force that the stairwell became a slaughterhouse—Eddie's blood, organs, and flesh hurled against the walls and stairs in a violent spray. Nearly split apart, he lay in ruin, and the haze of gun smoke lingered like Eddie's blood—an unyielding stain that refused to fade.

The article mentioned where his funeral had been held—Cummings and Davis. I contacted them, and they sent me his death certificate. Until then, I hadn't known the details of his death. Now I couldn't unknow them.

That's when the search turned serious. I knew Cleveland. I knew the East Side was where most Black families lived. So I got an Ohio Bell telephone book and started calling every Elkins on the East Side.

Eventually, I reached my Aunt Annette. I told her who I was, and she said, "Well, if Eddie's your father, you've got a big family."

Not long after, they flew me to Cleveland. At the gate, a banner read: *Welcome Home, Antwone.*

My Uncle Raymond—my father's brother—lived just two streets over on Hampton, near where I'd grown up on Drexel. Another brother, Uncle Spinoza, was close too—on East Boulevard off 105th, less than a mile from the foster home. That was the same part of Glenville where my father had lived when he died.

On my way to FDR Junior High, I'd walked past his apartment building almost every day, drawn to it—never knowing it had been his home.

Later, I got my father's death certificate, signed by my grandfather—Horace. Wow, I thought. I had a grandfather named Horace.

I came across my father's death certificate again and noticed the address. I typed it in—the place my grandfather had raised him—into Google Earth, and it took me straight to that same apartment building on Parkwood Drive. The same building I'd passed as a boy, not knowing.

And apparently, I'd gone to Parkwood Elementary School with some of my cousins—children I never knew were family.

One evening at my Uncle Spinoza's house, I met my sisters for the first time. After the tragedy, Frances had moved away, but Spinoza kept a hand out to them, slowly earning her trust.

That night Renee and Pamela came. I liked them right away. One was my age—we called each other twins, same father, different mothers. She asked me to spend the night, and our older sister, twenty months ahead of me, was going too.

Aunt Jannette slid into the front seat beside Renee. Pamela and I sat in the back.
She turned to look at me and hesitated.

Then Aunt Jannette said,

"I can't believe you're going to spend the night at the house of the people who killed your father."

That lit the fuse. Pamela—just four months old when our father was killed, Renee only eighteen months, and me still two months from being born—exploded, yelling and crying. Chaos filled the car. I jumped out and ran back to Spinoza's, told them what happened. They came out and calmed everything down. The irony was that Aunt Jeanette herself had once killed a man—under almost the same conditions as Frances—by severing an artery in his leg with a paring knife, right there in the kitchen of her east-side Cleveland apartment.

One just born, one barely toddling, one not yet here—suddenly left without a father.

I learned my sisters had never been told their mother killed our father. She and her husband smeared Eddie, accusing them of being "just like your father" whenever they did something wrong. It was more than just a lie—it was a way of making them carry a blame that never belonged to them, a cruel weapon used to hurt both Eddie's memory and his children. They grew up with that burden, not even knowing the truth. Eddie was stolen twice—once in life, then in memory. All the while, they were told he'd died in a car accident.

Some of my father's siblings held their anger for decades, honoring my grandmother Emma, who said, "Eddie's babies are going to need the whole family." So they carried it quietly, even as it burned inside them.

When I showed up with my father's looks, manner, and expressions, it was too much for Aunt Jannette. The anger she aimed at my twin really belonged to her mother—Frances Holden, who admits taking Eddie's life has haunted her ever since.

As a boy, I dreamed of that man in the graveyard often. I believed he was my father, though I could never quite see his face. Those dreams always took place in a graveyard—

long before I had ever heard he was dead. As if some part of me already knew the truth—that he was gone.

Later that night, I went to their house. I was sitting and talking with my twin's husband when I noticed an older woman in the kitchen. She was staring at me. Something in me knew—it was her. Frances Holden—the woman who had murdered my father, Eddie, when she was nineteen. I turned to look again—she was still staring, unblinking.

That must be her, I thought. Frances Holden.

She looked uncomfortable—but she had come anyway. Maybe she wanted to see me. Maybe it was her way of facing something. Maybe the last time she saw our father was the day he died—and now, here he was again, in me, walking into the kitchen from another room.

She sat nervously. I walked toward her… and said hello. Her eyes widened.

And that's where I'll leave that.

But I think she's been living in a nightmare for sixty-six years. Carrying something like that, decade after decade, is its own prison. Forgiveness doesn't excuse her, but I think she's due relief.

My Mother

I don't know if I'd ever seen my mother before the day I met her at thirty-three years old. But I've always carried a faint memory—uncertain, but real—of a visit to the Children's Center. My foster mother had taken me and Dwight there. A social worker brought me into a room where a young woman was waiting. She seemed older than a teenager, but not yet grown. She watched me closely. I had a toy truck in my hands, and when Dwight reached for it, she stepped in—pulled something else from the big wooden toy box and handed it to him. "Leave him alone," she told him. I noticed that. I remember looking at her and wondering, *Who is she?*

Years later, when I ordered my child welfare records, I found a note about that visit. It hadn't been a dream. But even then, I couldn't recall her face.

I also remember a box arriving at the house once. It was filled with new clothes. My foster mother opened it, gave Dwight a few things, and said it came from my mother. Likely through child welfare, because she wouldn't have been allowed to know where I was. But still—it came.

After Valencia told me we were foster kids, I began to wonder: Who is my mother? Where is she? Over time, those questions shifted to my father, too—neither of whom I had met. About my mother—so much was stacked against her. The heavy inheritance of Black existence in America. Her own mother died when she was just thirteen. Her father was already an alcoholic, unreliable, and her siblings were all older, off in the world on their own. She was left without the bond and guidance of family—placed into foster care, meandering through life before she was even seventeen. She tried to find her way. But she couldn't.

Years later, before I wrote *Finding Fish*, I started searching for my father's family. My uncle Spinoza told me he'd spoken with his friend Jess Fisher, who had a sister named Eva. Jess asked Spinoza to bring me by so he could "take a look."

That's how Black families used to decide—before DNA tests. You brought in the oldest relative, had them size you up, and say whether you belonged.

I eventually took the test, and not long after I was in a car with Uncle Jess and Uncle Spinoza—on my way to meet my mother. She lived in the Longwood Housing Projects, the same place I had passed through years earlier as a homeless teenager.

We entered through the kitchen. Jess first, then Spinoza, then me. A woman stood at the stove stirring food. I looked at her and thought, *That can't be my mother*.

But it was.

Jess asked who I was. She didn't know. She thought I was someone else. "That's Johnny," she said. "No," Jess told her who I was. "That's Antwone Fisher. Who's Antwone Fisher, Eva?"

Startled, she said, "My firstborn child."

I wasn't shocked so much as surprised. This was the person I had wondered about as a boy, imagined in so many ways. But the reality was different.

She sat down, overwhelmed. Then got up. Asked my uncle if I wanted something to eat. Looked at Spinoza instead of me. When I said no, she sat back down. Then suddenly ran out of the room. Jess followed, came back, and said, "There's nothing going on here. We better go."

Back at Spinoza's, my twin aunts Annette and Jannette asked me not to be angry. But I wasn't. I didn't feel anything at all. When I saw my mother, she was just a stranger—just someone I happened to be looking at. No magical connection. No reunion. Just somebody.

Later, she called me—after getting my number through Jess—two weeks after I returned to Los Angeles.

I asked her, "Why didn't you ever come for me?"

She said, "The truth is, Q… I just didn't want you." She called me Q—short for Quentin, my middle name.

At first I felt a spark of anger. But then I thought, *You asked. She answered. Don't get upset about it.*

As our conversations went on, I began asking her more. "What about my father?" I said. My first impression was that she hadn't really known him—maybe only casually. When I asked about his murder, she said she didn't know the girl who killed him. Then she added, *"You never know what went on between them. I've been in situations with a man where something like that could have happened while trying to protect myself. So I can't speak on it any more than that."*

We talked now and then. But slowly the calls faded, until there was nothing left to say. We'd asked every question. What remained was silence.

I saw her a few times in Cleveland. She wanted me to be angry, I think. Once, when I stepped outside, she confronted LaNette and said, "He's a chicken. He ought to just get it off his chest."

LaNette told her, "I don't think he's angry. I think he likes you."

She didn't believe that. She caused a fuss until they took her home.

I realized then she must've been carrying a lot of guilt. I tried calling to tell her it was okay. But I don't think she ever believed me.

I wasn't angry. Maybe she thought if the roles were reversed, she would've been. But that wasn't me.

One day I got the call that she had passed away. They told me I was her next of kin—her closest living relative—and nothing could proceed without my signature. I thought, Wow. I'd never considered myself anyone's next of kin, outside of LaNette, Azure and Indigo.

But she was my mother.

And I was proud to sign those documents. It felt like a privilege to help lay her to rest.

Her life had been difficult, I learned. I didn't hold her at fault. Everybody's not capable. And there was nothing to forgive.

Even so, she was known in ways I never expected.

Nate, my childhood friend—the son of the owner of Parkwood Groceries—worked for UPS. For forty years he drove a route that included my mother's home in the Longwood Estates. Twice a month he delivered her medication. He told me later how she'd greet him kindly, her apartment spotless, the blues playing low, sometimes snapping her fingers to the rhythm, a glass of Wild Irish Rose nearby.

One day his supervisor at UPS told him, "You know who that is? That's Antwone Fisher's mother." He couldn't believe it. But he never told her he knew me. Never told me he knew her. He kept it as his quiet secret.

Not long after, another driver whose route also ran through her street came back to the office with the news that my mother had passed away. That's how Nate's supervisor found out. So when Nate came in later to pick up her package, the supervisor told him directly, "You know, Antwone Fisher's mother died today."

On his route, he drove down her street that day and saw the coroner and police activity and their vehicles parked outside.

He said it felt sad and hollow, and he thought about me—knowing that I would hear the news soon. Because to him she was always "just a nice, cool lady who loved her blues and snapped her fingers to the groove. But more than that—she was my childhood friend's mother."

That's how he remembered her.

And this is how I remember her: as my mother.

Not perfect. Not imperfect. But still my mother.

The truth is, I never had the chance to learn what a mother really means—that special closeness so many people talk about. I know I'm supposed to have that, but it's like a fence I can't see through, keeping me from ever touching it.

It's a complicated feeling. There's a spiritualness about it that I recognize, but no history to hold on to. Like reaching for something you can never quite touch.

That's the saddest part about being in a situation where a parent isn't there. When they're gone, you know you'll never have that chance.

But the chance I did have was that I got to meet her.

And I did like her. We'd hug, and I held her close in my arms—

and in my eyes.

But it is my mind that holds her still,
the one who birthed me into the world... Eva Mae.

The Dream That Held Me

They Knew My Name

There was a dream I carried through my earliest years—a dream I never told anyone because it felt too sacred, too comforting, too real to risk being misunderstood.

I was a little boy, standing in a wide, open field of tall grass,
dressed in a heavy cotton shirt and burlap-style pants.
Then—suddenly—I was standing at the great barn doors.

They flew open.

And before me stood a man so tall I had to look up, I could see right into his nostrils.
He stood with his hands on his hips like he'd been waiting for me.
And he said my name:
"Antwone."

He knew me.

He brought me in, and a woman came and took my other hand.
Together, we walked inside.

All around us, high in the rafters and along the walls, people dressed like us whispered,
"It's Antwone... It's Antwone."

Not in fear. Not in ridicule. In recognition.

We walked toward a long table overflowing with food.

Pancakes.

Jelly.

Honey.

Things I loved as a child—things I could taste even in the dream.

And I sat and ate, while all the people watched with warmth,

as if I were someone they'd been waiting to return.

I had this dream from the time I was about two until around eight.

It comforted me through the worst of days.

When the real world was too hard, I'd close my eyes and try to find it—

like tuning a dial to a memory of being loved.

Sometimes it came.

Sometimes it didn't.

But when it did, I woke up full. Seen. Known.

Now I understand what I couldn't then:

this wasn't just a dream.

It was a shelter.

A place my soul created—or returned to—

when the world gave me none.

They knew my name there.

And in knowing it,

they gave me the strength to carry it until I could speak it for myself.

Down in Mississippi

Before we ever set out for Mississippi, I was just a boy on DuPont Avenue—a cobblestone street in Cleveland that sang beneath the wheels of every passing car. The sound of it came up through the floorboards and rattled inside your chest like bones in a box.

The houses along our street were a mix of A-frames and duplexes—some side by side, others stacked one on top of the other. Ours was the second house off Leuer Avenue, across from what I called the rock pile.

It wasn't really a pile—just a gravel parking lot for factory workers who came from all over the city. They'd park their cars, cross the street, and vanish into a big red-brick industrial building that smelled like burnt metal.

Behind our backyard stretched a thicket of slender trees and brush, separating the houses from a row of diesel truck repair shops and small factory warehouses along Leuer Avenue.

Past that was an open field where my friends and I caught grasshoppers in jars, and farther still lay the broad steel railroad tracks.

Just beyond the tracks, down the embankment, ran the I-90—the Cleveland Memorial Shoreway freeway—which eventually gave way to the powerful expanse of Lake Erie.

At night, the heavy locomotive would pass through—black, long, breathing smoke and steel. It shook the whole house like thunder. I could feel it in my bed. I almost knew, even in sleep, to stir just before it arrived. It was like a familiar ghost rumbling past the window. And it comforted me.

Cleveland in those years was a steel town.

The mills, the trains, the factories, the smell in the air—

the atmosphere a child grew up inside.

I didn't know it then, but my foster father had left Mississippi under a shadow. He'd been practicing his skill as a podiatrist and, for a time, had cared for the feet of an older white woman. When she passed away, the police found some of his homemade concoctions for her foot ailments, along with prescription medicines from her doctor. They arrested him, and when the ordeal was finally over, he packed up his family and joined the Great Migration, heading north to start anew.

By the time I came along, he'd built a life in Cleveland, far removed from whatever troubles had once sent him north. He worked steady for the Yoder Company—an outfit that made parts for big industries like automotive and aerospace. I never knew exactly what he did there—he wasn't an engineer or anything like that—but he retired from there after years of steady work and received a gold watch.

In his bedroom closet were stacks of old Louis Armstrong records that I never knew him to listen to. Maybe they were relics of his younger life. Now he was a preacher, a man of God. He'd carved out a quiet world for himself and my foster mother, well away from Mississippi.

Still, in the dark hours before dawn, he'd sometimes lie awake around four o'clock, listening to a radio program called *The White Folks Party*—a racist talk show that echoed the stations of Hattiesburg and Laurel, Mississippi. I imagine it brought back more than just voices. It brought back the air, the weight of the place he'd once called home—a place where, at the end of his life, he would return for good.

But we were about to head back down to Mississippi—not that I understood any of this at the time. Those stories would come to me slowly, piece by piece, years later.

That night was no different. I'd been called in early from the rock pile. The summer sun was still out, and I didn't know why bedtime was coming so soon. The bathwater was already running when I went upstairs—

started by someone older, maybe my foster sister. I turned it off, washed, and climbed into bed.

Later that night, the big black iron locomotive came through—moving along the tracks like a fire-breathing dragon, powerful and relentless, bearing steel. I woke just before the walls began to rumble, felt its familiar presence, and let sleep take me again.

The next thing I knew, my foster mother was shaking me awake.

"Get up," she said. "We have to go. We're going to Mississippi."

I'd heard of Mississippi, but I didn't know how far it was. I didn't know about the deep South.

I got dressed and stood in the living room with my foster brother Dwight. My foster mother and father were moving food into the trunk—roasting pans and foil-wrapped containers, trays that smelled like fried chicken and cornbread. I had no idea why so much food was going with us. But I remember thinking if all that food was for us, Mississippi must be a long way from here. We piled into the car in the dark and headed toward the Ohio Turnpike.

At night, that turnpike felt eerie. Lights in strange colors—amber, green, white—made the road look like something from outer space. I pressed my forehead against the glass and watched them blur past until sleep took me again.

Before I knew it, we were in Kentucky. A sign welcomed us with a picture of a man in a coonskin cap—Daniel Boone. The trees were taller. Everything was greener. And then we were back on the open road, cutting through rock walls and winding through mountain passes, the roads carved clean by machines.

Eventually, we crossed into the Magnolia State—Mississippi. The landscape changed again—more open, more flat. The houses grew fewer and farther between. One home every mile, maybe two. The roads were red clay. The air was different.

That was Mississippi.

The moment I stepped out of the car in Laurel, I knew I wasn't in Cleveland anymore. The air was quiet—no factories, no graphite grease, no steel trains spewing smoke. It was the first time I'd ever smelled what people would call "fresh air." I didn't know to call it that yet. I just knew it wasn't laced with the odor of an industrial city.

The house we arrived at was small, with a narrow porch just wide enough for two chairs. My foster mother's sister, Aunt Stella, lived there. The two of them embraced like time had been long. There was joy in the room—grown folks laughing and crying and holding on to each other. I stood back and watched.

My foster father went on to Hattiesburg and lodged with his own family. We stayed in Laurel with Aunt Stella.

When I was brought in to meet her, I noticed something sitting on her nightstand: a small black revolver with a white pearl handle.

Just sitting there in the open. It looked like a toy gun.

Aunt Stella seemed too old to be playing with toys.

As mischievous as I could be, I knew better than to touch it, so I looked away.

Our days there passed slow. There were no parks. No big group of neighborhood kids. No games in the street. Just me and my foster brother. The water came from a well and tasted like something I'd never had before. It wasn't bad—it was just different. Maybe that's how water's supposed to taste. And there was no bathroom in the house. Just an outhouse out back, which scared me more than a little.

Sometimes we'd take rides with my foster mother to visit friends or old relatives. One visit took us to a house that looked like a barn—long and high off the ground. When you stepped inside, you could see clear from the front door to the back. No rooms, just space. It was what people called a shotgun house—the kind of place where, they said, if you fired a shotgun through the front door, the shot would fly clean out the back into the wide open field without hitting a thing inside.

There were kids there, sleeping on pallets on the floor—blankets laid out in a row. I didn't see much furniture. I didn't even see a kitchen. But food was being made, and people were getting by. Eventually, it was time to head back to Cleveland. We packed the car again, just like before.

And this time, I understood something: the food in the trunk wasn't just for convenience. It was necessity.

We were traveling through a part of the country where certain places weren't meant for us.

That's why the food came with us. And that's why my foster mother carried *The Negro Motorist Green Book*, by Victor H. Green—a guide that told Black travelers where it was safe to sleep, to eat, to simply be.

She reached for it again and again, flipping through its pages, then setting it down—her hands resting on top of it, her head against the passenger-side window as she drifted off to sleep while we headed north, back to Cleveland.

Nowadays, some folks like to pretend that legal segregation was something from a long time ago. But it wasn't. It was legal in my lifetime. And truth be told, some would argue it's still stitched into the fabric of this country.

I didn't understand the depth of that at the time. But later, I would.

The ride home didn't feel as long as the ride down. Maybe it was because I knew where we were headed wasn't a mystery. It was home... Glenville... Cleveland. Familiar.

I had no idea how much that trip would change me.

I had heard of Emmett Till. I knew he'd been killed—accused of wolf-whistling at a white woman. That was all I really knew at the time—a boy who was killed for it somewhere in Mississippi.

It never entered my mind on the trip. How could I have known we had been just over a hundred miles from where he was kidnapped and murdered?

And only two hundred miles from where my father's side of the family had been held as slaves in Grenada, Mississippi—where my great-great-grandparents John and Sarah Jolliff lived and died.

But after we got back, I told my social worker all about the trip. I was excited. I thought she'd be glad to hear it.

"We went to Mississippi," I said.

And suddenly, everything changed.

She asked more questions. And then she asked to speak to my foster mother outside. From the window, I could see them on the porch. Her voice was low but serious. Firm. Concerned.

She wasn't angry at me. I wasn't in trouble. But I'd been taken somewhere I shouldn't have been. I was a ward of the state of Ohio. The state was responsible for my safety.

And the truth was, they'd never imagined someone would take a boy like me down to Mississippi—a place still haunted by killings.

Not just Emmett Till's—there were so many others during the Jim Crow years. Emmett was the one people talked about—but he wasn't the only one.

The social worker never finished her sentence.

"If something had happened to Antwone down there..."

But she didn't have to. Everyone knew about Mississippi.

A year later, on April 4, 1968, I was sitting in front of the television when the news broke: Dr. Martin Luther King Jr. had been shot.

I ran into the kitchen to tell the adults. The room cracked wide open—crying, shouting, people reaching for each other like the ground was trembling.

I was eight years old.

And I was there—alive and wide-eyed—when the world cracked again.

It had cracked open countless times before I was born.

But for me, these were the moments I began to see the cracks.

The Day I Got Humbled

I was in the ninth grade. Well—technically—it was my first day back after eighth. At the start of every school year, it was smart to reestablish yourself as a good fighter.
I was standing in the main hallway with some of my boys when a seventh grader—brand new to the school—walked in. He looked fresh. Nervous. Perfect.

I figured I'd pick on him to remind everybody that Antwone still had them hands. I took off the chain around my neck, swung it in a circle, and cracked him in the back of the neck as he walked past.

He spun around, mad.

I said, "What are you gonna do about it?" Then I told him I was gonna beat him up on Friday.

All week, he tried to avoid me—ducking into classrooms, hiding in crowds. I kept yelling, "I'm gonna get you Friday!" By the end of the week, the whole school was buzzing.

Then Friday came. We stood in the center of a crowd, facing off. Before I could even square up, he came at me fast. I stumbled, the crowd closed in, and I yelled, "Hey! Stop helping him!"

"Antwone," my friend said, "ain't nobody helping him. That boy's whuppin' your ass."

By the time he was done, I was exhausted. Wore out. Didn't get a lick in. My reputation? Gone.

A couple of weeks later, I broke my elbow in the most ridiculous way.

Back then, there was a TV show called *Kung Fu*, and the day after it aired, the hallways turned into our dojo. One day, I spotted my friend Melvin—big, strong, gentle. We started sparring, laughing. I surprised him with a clean kick to the chest. Everybody saw it.

He wasn't letting that slide. I tore down the hall, laughing, and rounded the corner at full speed. I leapt down four steps, glanced back midair to see how close Melvin was—and landed facing a wall I couldn't stop from hitting. I threw out my arms and slammed full force. My left elbow popped backward.

I knew it was bad. Melvin's laughter echoed in the background as a crowd began to gather. Mr. Glover, the gym teacher, came over, took one look at my arm, and said, "It looks disfigured." Not exactly what I wanted to hear.

Melvin shouted, "That's what you get!"

The vice principal sent me home, but by the next day the pain had only gotten worse. Mercy's father finally took me to Forest City Hospital, and from there I was transferred to Rainbow Babies & Children's. My arm was too swollen for surgery, so they propped it up and waited for the swelling to go down.

The next afternoon, they wheeled in a new patient—the seventh grader. He'd just had his appendix removed. When his family left that night, the nurses brought in fruit cups.

"What happened to you?" he asked.

"I broke my arm. You?" I said.

"My appendix busted. They had to take it out," he muttered.

And just like that, the wall between us started to fall. Over the next few days, we actually became real friends.

A couple of months later, Melvin—the one I'd kicked in the chest—broke his leg in a football game. When we all went to visit him—one look at me, saw me smiling, he yelled, "What are you doing here? You gotta go—no, for real, man, you gotta go. You're bad luck!"

He meant it, too.

But the day I got beat up by a seventh grader was a wakeup call. I learned not to judge by size or anything superficial, and not to bully.

It turned out we lived in the same direction, and every now and then we'd walk home together. By the end of the year, I found myself thinking, *I'm going to miss him when I graduate.*

The boy I once picked on.

The one who humbled me in front of the whole school.

My Social Workers

I remember a few of my social workers. Not all thirteen. But a few left something behind in me that stayed. The first I can truly remember was Ms. Jenkins.

A Black woman who wore what I call church lady hats—the kind with feathers, bows, flowers, satin, a stick pin with a pearl drop opposite the pointed end, and just enough pride to say: I still carry myself with dignity. Even in this world.

The last time I saw her, I was still a boy.

She came to visit me at the foster home on DuPont, as social workers were required to do. I didn't expect to see her that day, but when I stepped through the doorway to the enclosed porch, there she was—sitting on the old swing chair with that hat on her head like a crown.

She had retired by then, but she still wanted to see me.

She smiled when she looked at me and said, "My, haven't you gotten tall."

My foster mother stood near her, silent.

And then... the memory fades.

That porch furniture came from a white family on the West Side. My foster mother worked in their home, cooking and cleaning, and when they got new porch furniture, they gave the old set to her. That's how things came into our lives back then—hand-me-downs from places we'd never be invited to sit.

And then there was Ms. Neese.

I met her on a rainy school day while attending John Hay High School off Euclid Avenue. That day, I walked into the child welfare office a few miles down the same street. I didn't know her. She didn't know me. But the receptionist buzzed her to the front to find out what I was doing there. When she asked, I said, my foster mother told me, "Go back where I came from."

I had never met this woman in my life, but when she took me into her cubicle and opened my file, my story began to unlock.

She was the first person who ever told me my father's name—Edward Elkins and told me he had been killed two months before I was born. She was the first person to show me the newspaper article about his murder, reported in the *Cleveland Call & Post*—Cleveland's oldest Black community newspaper.

She told me my middle name—Quenton. I later learned from my mother that she gave me that name for a boy she liked when she was in elementary school. Ms. Neese told me other things too, things I never knew about myself.

At the time, I had no idea what that moment would come to mean. She told me my mother had been incarcerated when I was born—just a teenager herself, held in what they used to call a "girls' industrial school." Her mother had died when she was thirteen. Her father was unreliable, given to drink. And my father—murdered two months before I was born by a woman he'd had children with. A blast from a shotgun that nearly split him in two.

That day, I went from being a boy with questions to a boy with a story.

And Ms. Neese didn't just file my papers. She took me in.

Looked after me while I was in the children's center, until I was placed in reform school.

Years later, when the film *Antwone Fisher* was released, she reappeared in my life like she'd never left. These days, she usually checks in with LaNette. I guess most people know I still get shy, maybe a little standoffish. I don't even know why. That's just how I am.

But Ms. Neese has stayed.

From when I was fourteen to now—still looking after me.

Even at this age, it touches something deep in me.

Mercy

In the mid-60s, at the DuPont house. The house itself was a character in my story—now long gone, demolished after years of decay and time. It stood just a few miles from Lake Erie, close enough that in summer the wind would carry the lake's scent across the freeway, over the heavy tracks of massive, black, powerful locomotives that hauled steel and other industrial goods from the city to points across the country.

From there, the echo rumbled on, carrying the scent across a grassy field and over Leuer Avenue, drifting past the factories before slipping into our open windows. It carried with it the smells of graphite grease, steel, and water—a mix that settled into the house and into the rhythms of our lives.

The attic had been turned into a bedroom for the twin daughters of my foster parents. That's where Mercy and her sister slept. I didn't go up there often, but one winter afternoon, I did.

They were playing music, getting ready to go out—maybe skating or to a friend's house. I sat in a chair near the dresser, watching a portable record player on top of it. It looked like a small suitcase, its speakers swinging open on the sides, revealing a turntable laid out flat, with a tall spindle in the center for stacking 45s. When one record finished, the next would drop into place, and the arm would lift and settle softly onto it. The music would play. I was fascinated by the whole thing.

One of the songs that dropped and played that day was *Are You Lonely for Me Baby* by Freddie Scott. I loved it instantly. I asked Mercy to play it again, and she did. Her sister had gone downstairs, and for a moment it was just me and Mercy. Then she left too—but she left the record playing so I could hear the song again.

She was always kind like that. Gentle. She had a sweetness that never went away. I think she might've been eleven or twelve—maybe just a little older at the time. We were just kids. But she carried herself like someone who saw things other people didn't see. Including me.

She was a teenager when I was a child. I remember her and her sister coming home from school, walking in with their Glenville jackets and those spiral notebooks with the Tarblooder on the cover. They'd sit at the table and write in cursive—something I couldn't do yet. I couldn't even tell time. She said she'd teach me both.

I only remember her really getting upset with me once. I hadn't dressed myself properly, and she scolded me for it. Maybe she thought I should've known better by then.

But even in that moment, there was no cruelty. By the next time I saw her, she was the same as always—there wasn't a trace of lingering anger.

I remember her taking Dwight and me on the bus one day, both of us dressed in our little church clothes. I didn't know where we were going. We rode up 105th, and next thing I knew, we were in a house with a pool table. I didn't realize it then, but looking back, I think it may have been the house of a boy she liked. While she visited with him, Dwight and I rolled the balls around the table, laughing and playing. Later we got back on the bus and returned home like it was nothing.

Mercy always said yes. Every Friday in the summer, when she got her paycheck, Valencia and Dwight would coach me to ask her for money—"Just a quarter," they'd say. "Fifty cents." And she always gave it to me. She was the first person I remember giving me a holiday gift—a tomato-red pullover sweater shirt with mustard stripes down the arms. She got Dwight one too: powder blue with navy stripes. I still remember it.

She grew up fast and carried herself with quiet confidence. I believe she trained as a key punch operator and started working right after high school. I never knew her not to have a job—sometimes two. One day she came to the Drexel house with a car dealer who was trying to sell her a brand-new, lime green Dodge Charger. They parked it in the driveway, and we all poured off the porch to look. It was a beauty. In the end, she decided it wasn't the right fit—probably too powerful—but I remember how she lit up looking at that car. She had style.

Years later, at age seventeen—after reform school, emancipated and on the street—her kindness showed up for me in a way I'll never forget. One day, Valencia ran into me at 105th and St. Clair, right in front of the Cleveland Trust Bank. I told her I was on the street, and without hesitation she told me to call Mercy. She was sure Mercy would help me—and she was right.

I walked to a telephone booth—it was the 1970s, and they were still everywhere—and dialed the number Valencia had given me. It was one of those late-season warm days, an Indian summer just before the cold set in. Mercy picked up and, in her easy way, invited me to come stay at her Sherwood Village townhouse in Bedford Heights.

She let me sleep on her sofa, asked me to watch her children when she went to work, and gave me money when she got paid. She bought a component stereo system—turntable, radio, separate speakers—because she knew how much I loved music. Not a little suitcase record player like the one she had as a teen. This one was grown-up.

I used it to play the albums I bought with the money she gave me—records I treasured, records her twin sister later took from me. And when I asked for them back, she refused. That's something I still haven't quite gotten over.

Aside from a few items of clothing, those records were my only possessions. Sometimes, it's the little things that matter most. It hurt—because it was all I had.

Eventually—after about four months—I began to realize that Mercy didn't owe me anything. I started making myself scarce—I could feel I was in the way. She never said so, but I knew it.

It was winter.

With nothing to pack, and no desire to explain, I left. I started couch-surfing again, and on December 23, 1977, I joined the Navy.

But I never forgot what she did for me that brisk fall in '77.

I haven't seen Mercy or her children in many years, but I hope their lives turned out well. And even if there were hardships, I know it wouldn't have been because they lacked a good mother. She was smart, hardworking, and loving.

Years later, I had another book published and returned to Cleveland for a signing at Joseph-Beth Booksellers. The line was long. I was signing one copy after another when someone from the store leaned in and said, "There's a woman who keeps getting to the front of the line, then stepping out and going to the back again. Do you know who she is?"

I looked over. And there she was.

Mercy.

Holding *Finding Fish* in her hands.

I hadn't seen her since I left her townhouse. When she finally stepped up to the table, I could see how nervous she was. Her neck was throbbing. She looked terrified. But her sweetness was still there, echoing. I don't know why I wasn't warmer to her. I regret that. She had always been warm to me.

I signed her book—I don't even remember what I wrote. Maybe a name her mother gave me. The one Mercy would remember.

I don't know what she expected from me. But I know what she gave me.

All those years I lived in that house—feeling unwelcome, hearing what people said about me—what was done to me. She was the one who made me feel seen. She didn't belong to the cruelty of that household, even though she lived in it. She was something softer. Something better.

She wasn't powerful—I'm sure she had no idea about the quiet, terrible things that went on in that house. But she was a light. A gentle one, steady and unassuming, that illuminated the path to the idea that there were good people in the world—people like her.

Sometimes, there are things you don't say out loud. You just leave them behind in the open, hoping the right eyes will see them. Like this:
Even the hardest earth learns light.
Look closely, and you'll see.

Valencia

Valencia was my foster sister. But really—she was my sister in every way that mattered. About four years older than me, she was always there—kind, constant.
She loved chocolate bars, and when she was sad, I'd find a way to get her one. She appreciated that. And I appreciated her.

We were close. In some ways, I felt closer to Valencia than Dwight was, though he was her biological brother. They argued a lot. Valencia and I had our arguments too—me saying things that made her mad or disappointed her—but we always found our way back. That was us: natural, sometimes rough, but real.

I must have been about six when *Going to a Go-Go* by Smokey Robinson and the Miracles was on the radio. It was one of those Cleveland winters when snow piled high and kept you inside. One quiet afternoon, Dwight and I sat in our room while Valencia came in pushing one of those old carpet sweepers—the kind that looked like a vacuum—and said, "Let's have a talent show."

We leaned against the chest of drawers under the window while Valencia stood with the carpet sweeper handle as her microphone and sang *Going to a Go-Go*. She wore a wool pleated skirt and sweater, dressed warm like we all did when the house couldn't keep the heat. When she finished, she told Dwight it was his turn. He wouldn't do it—just teased her. Then she told me to sing.

Bashful as I was, I sang *The Way You Do the Things You Do*, trying to sound like Eddie Kendricks of The Temptations. When I finished, Valencia said, "Wow, you can sing good." Dwight said I sounded like a girl—but he was just jealous.

Years later, Uncle Raymond told me my father sang falsetto with a Cleveland group called the Jive Kings. He said my father's voice was like Tony Williams of the Platters—a real compliment.

After that, I only sang around Dwight and Valencia. I'd lie on the floor with my feet on the heater vent and sing while Valencia listened from the doorway. It drove Dwight crazy, which only made me sing louder. One day she called me into the hall and said, "Don't listen to Dwight. You have a good voice—you could get famous." That was Valencia—always encouraging me.

I stayed shy about singing, but I never forgot that winter. And as the years passed, I watched Valencia grow into a young woman.

I remember sitting on the porch stairs, daydreaming. A boy from the neighborhood—maybe four or five years older than me—rode up on his bike and said, "Hey, how you doing?" Just small talk. Then, "Okay, I'll see you later."

I'd seen him around before. He seemed to pay me special attention, and I didn't understand why. Then he came by again. Valencia appeared in the doorway and stepped out with quiet confidence, like she'd been watching all along.

The boy took off fast—like he suddenly remembered somewhere else to be.
She asked, "Do you know him?"
I said, "No, but he keeps coming by. Do *you* know him?"
"Yeah," she said, nodding. "He likes me." As foster kids in that house, we always knew we weren't truly welcome. Still, Valencia tried to be part of that family. I watched her do her best. And still—ugly things were said and done to her.

Then one day, something different happened.

She'd been invited to model in an Avon fashion show. I didn't know the details, but on the day of the show I was walking down the street—and there she was, insouciant as ever.

In a gorgeous floral dress, with the sun pouring over her, she seemed to glow from within.

I walked up, and before I could say anything, she smiled and said, "Qué pasa, baby?"

I blinked. "What?"

She laughed. "¿Qué pasa?—it means 'What's happening?' in Spanish."

And in that moment—with the honeyed light on her satin-smooth, milk-chocolate skin, her shimmery Afro hairdo, and the poise that came so naturally to her—I stopped thinking of Valencia as just pretty.

She had a light that wasn't only seen, it was felt—like opening a window after a long winter, when the air rushes in fresh and full of promise.

I realized…

My sister was beautiful.

The 4th of July

And the Boy at the Gate

I woke up on the 4th of July at the DuPont house when I was about six years old. Sunlight poured through the bedroom window—it felt like a special day. The air already carried the scent of lighter fluid and charcoal through my open window. Families up and down our cobblestone street were getting ready to barbecue, celebrate, and wave their flags.

Interesting holiday to revere as much as they did. I didn't know then—couldn't know—that in 1776, Black people were still enslaved in the United States—when independence and freedom was declared. But like the good Americans they were trying to be, my neighbors celebrated anyway.

It was a fun day. Adults danced and laughed—the street was alive with children—from toddlers to teens. Some playing Simon Says, others jumping rope, hopscotch on the sidewalk, kickball in the grass. All the games the boys and girls loved to play together beneath the trees. I was too small to join in some of the games I wanted to, but I'd watch from the sidelines, taking it all in—with the celebratory sounds of music, and young and old lost in the joy of community, togetherness, and love.

And from nearly every porch or backyard, radios were tuned to the local Black station—WJMO, Super 1490 on your radio—in the best location in the nation. You'd hear the DJ say it with that signature voice, like a heartbeat of the neighborhood. That music, those sounds—they all hung in the air and made the day feel like magic.

My foster sister, Valencia, had a bike. A big one. It looked enormous to me—but I wanted to ride it more than anything. She always said no. I thought she was being selfish. I never thought she didn't want me to hurt myself. Treating me like a baby, I thought—and I didn't like it.

So I snuck it from the backyard, wheeled it down the driveway, and took off down the sidewalk. I stood on the pedals—I couldn't reach the seat. I coasted all the way down the block, toward the hill at the end of our street.

I was doing it—riding with confidence. I felt proud. I wished Valencia was watching me. She'd see she was wrong. At the bottom was a park and some basketball courts. I could hear the shouts of boys playing, the sound of the ball hitting pavement. Barbecue smoke hung in the air, and I was riding on that big old bike with no help.

Then I rolled through the park's parking lot and came to some broken glass near the curb. Worried the tire might go flat, I panicked. Tried to adjust. Tried to sit. Something went wrong. I lost control—and fell right into the glass.

A deep gash opened across my knee—it took a lot of stitches to close—now a scar, a reminder of that summer 4th of July. I must've screamed. One of the boys playing basketball saw me. He ran from the court, came up the embankment, and picked me up. I was bleeding badly. He asked where I lived. Through tears, I told him—up the street. He hoisted me over his shoulder, grabbed the bike with one hand, and carried us both all the way home. Blood covered him by the time we reached the porch. All the kids who saw him carrying me on his shoulder seemed to panic and followed us all the way to the house where I lived. The boy gently set me down and laid the bike on the grass.

Valencia was one of the first to run over to check on me. She never asked why I took the bike after she told me not to ride it. That was how she was. She probably felt I'd learned my lesson.

But no. Not me.

I could hardly wait to get back on that bike. And one day I did—riding up and down the sidewalk with everybody watching.

But I never forgot that boy.

His face is blurry now, like a shadow. But his kindness is sharp in my memory. That was the kind of neighborhood it was—where if you were doing wrong, a neighbor might straighten you out or call your house before you even got home. Where someone would stop their game to carry a hurt kid home, no questions asked.

He didn't know me. But he helped me.

The Voice Before the Sermon

The first thing my foster father did was take his place in the pulpit behind the lectern he built himself—suited and booted, ready with his well-worn opening line: "Wherever two are gathered in My name, there I will be also. So the Lord must be in here somewhere."
There were seven members of the church so far—present and accounted for.

I figured I'd better behave.

I don't want to give the impression that my foster father was a charlatan—he wasn't.

And there wasn't anything funny about the scene. It was very dramatic, very serious.

He was a deeply religious man, spiritual in his own way. He preached with his heart and soul—the only way he knew how. A sincere, hard-working man and a healer who used herbs and, at times, truly eased my suffering from eczema.

That part of him—the preacher, the caregiver—stood in stark contrast to how I was treated in his home otherwise.

I was just a boy, sitting in an empty row of hard foldout chairs—well, Dwight was seated next to me, buzzing on the verge of catching the Holy Ghost. He'd caught it once before, so I knew the signs when it was coming—and I was poised to get out of the way.

We were watching my foster father sweat and preach with a powerful fervor—like thunder and lightning wrapped in scripture. He was the pastor of his own seven-member Pentecostal storefront church, with display-case windows flanking a narrow foyer.

He'd covered each window in stained-glass contact paper, then carefully cut a Christian cross from the center. Behind the cutout, he placed a sheet of plain white paper, and on the display floor behind that, he set a small table lamp with a soft white bulb that glowed warmly in each window.

To passersby, the glowing cross created a holy scene—a quiet beacon calling the wretched inside to be saved.

My foster mother would get caught up in the spirit—speaking in tongues, shouting with her arms outstretched, rubbing her thighs and hips as if trying to soothe them, sometimes even taking off down the aisle between the foldout chairs.

When she was seated, she'd strike her big bass drum resting on the floor beside her, pounding it with her mallet. It made the whole scene feel even more dramatic—like heaven was cracking open.

There were times I'd be completely wrapped up in the sermon itself, listening close, when she'd suddenly hit that drum—and I'd shoot straight up out of my seat, heart pounding, thinking Judgment Day had arrived.

She'd look at me, wide-eyed, convinced the Holy Ghost had finally snatched me up out of my seat and was about to save me.

But that wasn't it.

I'd just gotten scared.

She and Mother Crump—the only other adult woman in the church—would dance, shout, and testify. Some of the others joined in too, even Dwight. At times, people were running around me like the Holy Ghost was jumping in and out of everybody.

But me—it left alone.

So I just sat there. Watching. Listening. Still.

I wasn't unmoved.

I was truly listening.
I was really watching.

Sometimes it crossed my mind—maybe the Holy Ghost just didn't like me. My foster mother once told me as much. She said that big day when Dwight caught it, because I didn't, I must be on my way to hell.

She didn't just imply it.

She said it.

And I believe she meant it.

It was all very distracting for me. I'd try to focus on one thing, and something else would happen—snatching my attention away. I was waiting for something I could recognize and hook into to rise up out of all that sound, fire, and brimstone raining down in that little storefront church on Woodland Avenue.

What I felt seemed deeper. Quieter. Older.

They were tuned to a high emotional pitch, it appeared.

I was tuned to a frequency they couldn't hear—one that didn't live in loudness, but in stillness.

The louder the noise, the quieter the voice inside me that wanted to share in the spirit.

The quieter things got, the louder and more discernible that voice became.

That's what it's always been for me.

Something in me always whispered:

listen closer to find the truth.

There was truth in that little church on Woodland Avenue—but I had to listen for it.

It wasn't rebellion on my part.

It was memory.

My ancient-ness was speaking.

Something older than pulpits, older than sermons—was humming its truth.

And I eventually heard it.

Even as a child.

It's taken me a lifetime to give that feeling a name. To realize what I carried wasn't disconnection.

It was discernment.

I was born on a different frequency—one meant for knowing, not just reacting. One meant for watching the fire, not just dancing in it.

And now, I honor that stillness.

That sacred hum beneath my skin.

I don't need noise to be close to spirit.

I don't need permission to feel what's true.

I was never lost.

I was just listening…

to the voice that came before the sermon.

Did You Read About Me?

When I was fourteen years old, I was removed from my foster home and placed at the Metzenbaum Children's Center, named after Ohio Senator Howard Metzenbaum. It was an orphanage and a kind of temporary way station—for kids being transported elsewhere or waiting for placement, like I was.

The kids came from all kinds of circumstances. Since the school at the center didn't go up to high school, I attended East Tech nearby and walked back and forth each day. The facility wasn't meant for long stays, but I ended up staying more than seven months.

There was a woman who worked the evening shift—Mrs. Brown. A lovely Black woman. Warm. Steady. I didn't talk much during that time. I'd been through a lot and spent most of my time lost in daydreams. Mrs. Brown sat in a chair at the head of the boys' corridor, watching over the common area where the younger kids played. The building was shaped like a wagon wheel, with four corridors like spokes—one for younger boys, another for older girls, and so on.

I used to sit on the floor beside her. She might've been knitting or crocheting—doing something with her hands.

And she'd talk. Mostly about her son. It was clear how much she loved him. I remember the way her voice changed when she spoke of him—how proud she was. I used to think, *I wish I had a mom who could be proud of me like that.* Her son, I believe, was a linebacker for the Philadelphia Eagles.

I imagined she was my mom—bragging to some kid like me about me.

One day, caught up in all that imagining, I blurted out, *One day, you're gonna read about me.*

She paused. Looked at me. And I could see the doubt on her face.

She said, *Well, I hope it'll be for something good.*

I didn't say anything after that. I tried to hide the disappointment on my face. I wasn't her son. And maybe, given my circumstances, she couldn't picture someone like me making it. She didn't mean any harm. But I never forgot that look.

Years later, I wrote my memoir and had become Antwone Fisher—to some degree.

Years later, I was at a bookstore in Shaker Heights, Ohio, signing copies of my book *Finding Fish: A Memoir*.

A woman walked up to my table with what we in the Black community call a *Kool-Aid smile*—so wide and sweet it caught my attention. I thought, *What is this lady grinning about?*

"You don't remember who I am, do you?" she asked.

I said, "Sorry. No, I don't. "I'm Mrs. Brown," she said. "I worked at the Children's Center."

And it hit me like a sudden gust of wind that came out of nowhere. Before I could take another breath, I smiled and said, "Did you read about me?"

"Yeeees, baby," she said, nodding with pride. "I read about you. I was so proud."

I gleamed with pride myself. "I told you," I said. It was hard to imagine that her Kool-Aid smile could have grown any whiter, but it did.

Mr. Nobody

A night on the street

Summer of 1977.
Warm nights, long days—and nowhere to go.
There were other kids who had aged out of foster care like I had—some of them out on the streets, too. Almost from day one, I saw how desperate some had become. They talked about getting money—mostly through crime. I understood why. Even me. Like Oliver Twist, I had my own Fagin.

My friend Leslie, from the orphanage, had also aged out that summer. He went down the wrong road fast. It felt like looking into a mirror—and I probably looked just as desperate. But I knew I didn't want that life. Not for me.

So I made a choice. I left the area. I thought maybe if I went back to Glenville—the neighborhood I knew—someone there might help. Maybe someone would remember me. That felt better than becoming someone I wasn't—or losing my life out there.

Most people didn't believe I was homeless. They figured I had somewhere to sleep. But I didn't. No home. No guarantees. Sometimes I could talk a friend into letting me sleep in a basement or on the floor in their bedroom—

but not always. Especially not after I left the men's shelter. Truth is, I escaped it. There's one night I remember clearly. It might've been August. The air was warm, but I was shivering—not from the cold, but from fear. From loneliness. I didn't understand it then. I only knew I couldn't stop shaking.

When I got back to Glenville, the first thing I wanted to know was whether my old foster family still lived in that big Victorian on Drexel—just two doors from Parkwood. But I was too afraid to go near it. I circled the block, hoping to spot a familiar car. I saw a truck, but I wasn't sure if it was my foster father's. I stayed away. And every time a car came up behind me, I'd glance over my shoulder, heart racing, worried someone might recognize me. I didn't want to be seen like that.

I walked for hours, sticking close to what I knew. The storefronts were full of rats, broken glass, and the stink of plaster and urine. I kept moving, hoping the familiar might protect me.

The silence was eerie. Crickets chirped louder than I ever remembered. No birds. No music. No cars. Just a hollow kind of quiet. I watched windows glowing behind curtains—tiny signs of life that made me feel a little less alone. But one by one, those lights went out. And with each one, the neighborhood darkened—not just in light, but in spirit.

Now and then, a car passed in the distance. I called them the night people. Folks who moved through the dark for reasons I couldn't guess—and probably didn't want to. Once, I saw someone dart across the street, low and fast, like they didn't want to be seen. And sometimes a police cruiser would ease down Parkwood Drive, headlights low. Not rushing. Just watching. But it didn't make me feel safer.

I had a knowing—the kind you don't learn, just feel. The danger of the night. I couldn't see it, but I felt it pressing in, heavy and present. Maybe that's why I was shaking. The fear wasn't loud—but it never left.

I ducked into a storefront foyer, knees to my chest, head down. I sang songs in my mind to pass the time. But the minutes dragged. I thought about food. About a hot bath. About friends. But mostly, I just sat there—trying to make it through.

Then, out of nowhere, a soft, cool breeze swept into the foyer like a street sweeper's brush and whirled around me —and through me. And in my mind, it spoke:

I'm cleaning the night air. What's your excuse?

It startled me—but it also felt like a blessing. Like even the wind knew I didn't belong out there. Then morning came—but not the kind I was hoping for.

Instead of sunrise, a thick fog rolled in from Lake Erie. It wrapped around everything, swallowing up the houses and streets. I couldn't see more than a few yards ahead. The world was still hidden—like night didn't want to let go. I felt trapped. Imprisoned by fog. I couldn't move forward—couldn't see a way out. I ached for the fog to lift—so I could return to the world again. And then a car appeared through the mist. Slow and ghostlike. At first, I was just glad to see another human being. After such a long night, the sight of life moving again gave me hope. As it came closer, I tried to see the driver. I wanted them to see me, too.

And when our eyes finally met—it was just a passing glance—but it cut through me. It said everything:
What are you doing out here this early in the morning?

That one look burned. I felt exposed. Not just homeless—ashamed. Ashamed to be standing there at all. In the fog. On an empty street where no kid should have been.

It was the kind of shame that makes you think someone can see all your secrets at once. I felt like that driver knew everything—that I was hungry, unwashed, alone... that I had been found asleep on bedroom floors—at one friend's house or another—and put out into the night more times than I care to remember. Once it was on Michael Williams' bedroom floor—sent back out into the morning with nowhere to go.

And I hated that feeling. I wanted to disappear back into the fog.

Eventually, the fog lifted.

And I could see—I was still in the world.

Way to Come Back Home!

Part 1: My First Achievement

When I left the orphanage at 14, I was placed in a reform school—what they called them back then—in western Pennsylvania. I stayed there until I graduated high school at 17. That graduation was my first real achievement.

The morning after, I felt proud. Hopeful—maybe for the first time in a long time.

Then my social worker, Bill Ward, showed up at the door of my room.

"I'm here to take you back to Cleveland," he said.

I was stunned. I hadn't known I'd be leaving that day. I thought I'd have time to prepare.

"You're being emancipated," he told me.

"What does that mean?" I asked.

"I'll explain on the drive," he said.

So we got in the car and headed west. I don't remember much of what he said—his voice faded into the background. My mind was somewhere else. I stared out the window, watching the trees and pastures slide by under the open sky. I was daydreaming… and quietly hoping.

Hoping maybe I'd run into someone from my past—Freda, Janise, Jesse, Gary—Michael. Childhood friends who had once meant something real to me. Maybe they'd remember me.

Then Bill broke the silence.

"You listening?"

I turned to him. I guess my face gave me away, because he paused. Then he said they'd found a place for me—a men's shelter in Cleveland. I'd have a room there for two months. But once I turned 18, I'd be expected to pay for it myself.

"You'll need to get a job," he said. "Provide for yourself."

I was in shock.

No orphanage. No more foster homes. No one to help. It was the end of the road.

Who's going to do this for me? Who's going to do that for me? What about food? Clothes? What about tomorrow?

My mind was spinning.

Then he said something I never forgot: "Don't feel sorry for yourself. It doesn't do any good."

That set me aflame with anger.

I thought, *I can't feel sorry for myself?* Truth is, I had gotten good at it. Feeling sorry for myself had become a kind of comfort. And maybe I had reason to. But I was also approaching a time when that kind of thinking could become dangerous.

He dropped me off at a historic YMCA building in downtown Cleveland that had been converted into a shelter. I learned fast that it wasn't safe. There were predators of all kinds, and the energy inside that place made it impossible to stay. One thing led to another, and I ended up out on the street.

I started panhandling. Walking up to strangers. Asking for change.

Most just looked through me like—they've got their own problems.

I was on my own.

Part 2: Cleveland Trust

One day, in front of the old Cleveland Trust Bank at 105th and St. Clair, I saw a familiar face—a ray of hope. It was Valencia, my foster sister. She had grown into womanhood—modern, more beautiful than I remembered. Still satin-smooth and milk chocolate.
She could see I wasn't doing well.

She cared. Like always. She suggested that maybe one of our old foster sisters—the kind one I called Mercy in

Finding Fish, whose parents' home we had shared as foster children—might let me stay with her family for a while.

And she did.

I stayed for a bit—long enough to see I was in the way.

Eventually, I had to go. It was time.

And so it began again. Surfing couches. A few days at Michael Williams' house until his mother caught me and kicked me out. A stretch at Jesse Boston's.

None of them could believe my situation.

I was drifting.

Then—like a thunderclap—I heard it again. My social worker's voice:

"Don't feel sorry for yourself. It doesn't do any good."

And in that moment, I wished he was there. Not to argue. Not to complain.

But to tell him... as hard as it was to hear, he told me the truth. I realized he was right.

Feeling sorry for myself wasn't helping.

It was keeping me stuck. And slowly, something else became clear. I had always lived under someone else's roof—the foster homes, the orphanage, the reform school, even the shelter. Every place came with danger, abuse, or the risk of being told to leave.

That had to change. I needed something of my own. A place where no one could put me out.

That was the day I stopped waiting to be rescued.

The day I started thinking about what I could do for myself to survive.

Part 3: Way to Come Back

Years later, I was back in Cleveland—and I brought Hollywood with me.

We were filming *Antwone Fisher*.

One day, we were shooting a scene inside a small corner grocery store on 105th, just adjacent to Drexel, where I had once lived in the foster home. We had just finished a few takes when someone came in and said there was a man outside who wanted to speak with me.

We were on a break, so I walked through the store and stepped outside.

Across the street, behind a yellow line of police tape that kept onlookers at bay, a crowd had gathered.

That's when I saw him. A man waving his arms high above his head, shouting my name:

"Antwone! Antwone!"

I looked again.

It was Bill Ward—my old social worker. The one who had driven me back to Cleveland after reform school.

When he saw he had my attention, he cupped his hands around his mouth and shouted across the street: "Way to come back, Antwone! Way to come back home!"

CSU

When I got out of the reform school, they brought me back to Cleveland and placed me in a men's shelter. It used to be a YMCA, but by then it had been converted. I didn't want to be there. I'd come in late at night, just slip inside and try not to be seen. Then I'd get up real early and leave before anybody was moving around. I just didn't want people to see me. I was trying to stay out of sight.
But I had my own Fagin I ran into. That's what I called him —like from *Oliver Twist*. So I wasn't always successful at hiding.

One day I was walking around and ended up at Cleveland State University. It wasn't that far from the shelter. I don't even remember how I got there exactly. I just found myself on campus, and I liked it there. It was summer, so it wasn't packed with students, but there were some around. I thought maybe I could blend in.

Some of the students had cameras—Nikon, Canon—the kind with big lenses and those colorful, psychedelic straps hanging from their shoulders. It almost looked like part of their outfit, like a fashion piece. They looked like they belonged there. Me, I wasn't sure how I looked. I didn't know if I fit in. But I tried.

It became a kind of refuge for me. A place I could go and not feel so exposed. I could use the restroom, splash water on my face, sit down somewhere and just feel safe for a little while. I never really felt comfortable, not all the way. I felt like people could see I didn't belong. But I kept coming back.

And I started to imagine myself going there one day. Like maybe I could be normal like some of those students. I wished for that. I really did.

Eventually, I had to leave the downtown area for my own safety. But I still remember that summer. That moment in time when I found some peace just being around that campus.

And years later, I went back. Not to blend in, but to be honored. I gave the commencement address. CSU gave me an honorary degree. I wore the gown and the cap. My elementary school teacher, Ms. Profit, was there. LaNette was with me. Azure and Indigo were there, too.

It wasn't just a degree I was receiving—it was something more. It felt serendipitous. Like life had brought me full circle, and there I was, standing in the place where I once came just to feel safe.

And I held that big degree in my hands.
And I took pictures.

Pamela Louis

I met Pamela Louis in the summer of 1977—the same summer I was homeless. I was spending a lot of time with Michael Williams back then, and he introduced us at Randall Park Mall, a place that's long gone now. We were standing outside the Sam Goody record store when he spotted her.

I remember clearly: *Wishing on a Star* by Rose Royce was playing through a speaker just outside the entrance. That's how the stores drew people in—music floating into the mall, inviting you to step inside.

Michael and Pamela started talking, and I just stood there looking at her.

She was beautiful.

But it wasn't just that—there was something about the way she carried herself. Confident. Grounded. My foster brother would've said, "She doesn't fake the funk." And he would've been right. She had this easy, familiar way of talking that made you feel like you already knew her.

There were no cell phones back then. Before I left, she gave me her home number—the one at her mother's house, where she still lived. We were only seventeen.

That's how we stayed in touch after I went into the Navy. It turned out she lived in the Glenville neighborhood too—I just hadn't seen her before. I don't remember exactly how we exchanged numbers, but we must have met up several times before things got really crazy for me.

I had her address, and I wrote to tell her I'd joined the Navy and was in boot camp.

She started writing me letters—every week, sometimes twice.

Usually just a short note inside a card.

She loved Garfield, the orange cartoon cat, and most of her cards featured him.

Her messages weren't romantic—just friendly, encouraging. Something I needed more than I realized back then.

We became close—not in the can't-be-apart way, but in a solid, quiet kind of friendship. Some people think it's odd how a guy can be just friends with a pretty girl. But almost every girl I've ever been close to was beautiful. Including my wife LaNette.

But wait—hold on… maybe I'm just a pretty-girl magnet.

Or maybe there's something about me that makes pretty women feel safe.

Like a gift.

One time we met downtown and had lunch at a fast-food place. I'll never forget it. She asked me what I wanted, told me to go sit down, and then brought our food over on a tray. She opened a napkin, laid it out in front of me, and placed my order on it.

That small act—it stuck with me.

It made me feel seen.

Special.

I liked her. I won't pretend I didn't. If she'd ever leaned in that direction, I probably would've followed. But I didn't have anything to offer her. I was surfing sofas. And that wasn't the nature of our connection.

We were just... friends.

Once, I didn't know what to write, so I copied the Todd Rundgren song made popular in my neighborhood by the Isley Brothers:

"Hello, it's me, I thought about us for a long, long time..."

She wrote back, "That last letter sounded like a song I know."

I was embarrassed. But she just moved on—expecting me not to try that stuff again.

It wasn't a big deal.

That's Pamela.

Later, aboard my first ship, the USS *Schenectady* (LST-1185), I received one of her letters. When I opened it, a photo of her slipped out and landed on the table.

Eric, a shipmate and friend, picked it up and said, "Is this your girlfriend?"

I told him, "No. Just a friend."

He smiled and said, "I bet you marry a pretty girl."

And I did.

Over the years, Pamela and I stayed in touch. We became lifelong friends—the kind you only get a few of in this life. We've shared secrets, laughter, and losses.

These days, when I call, she answers the phone with, "Hi, lifelong friend."

And that's exactly what we are.

I was seventeen when I met her. She was too. And looking back, I realize something:

She held me up at a time when I had nothing—whether she knew it or not. Her kindness, her letters, her friendship... they gave me something solid to hold on to.

That's not simple.

That's everything.

You know...

I think I'll give her a call.

The Kiss

I've always joked that I must be some kind of pretty girl magnet. Somehow, they always found their way to me. And there it was again—right there on the Sony Pictures Studio lot, beneath the big clock that hangs off the Capra Building on Main Street.

That's where I first saw her.

She was wearing a blue dress, my favorite color. It clung gently to her form. Not loud or showy. Not asking for attention. It was the kind of dress you remember not because of what it revealed—but because of what it quietly suggested. There was something soft about seeing her that day. The whole moment felt hushed, like it didn't want to be interrupted.

She told me later that her sister had said, "You're going to meet your husband in that dress."

And she did.

Looking back, I think that dress might've been magic. Not because of how it looked—but because of what it stirred in me. Maybe it had that effect because it was supposed to have that effect. Probably. It felt like one of those moments life places in front of you to see if you're paying attention.

I called out, "Hey, Miss Fisher." She looked over and said, "My name is Canister." I nodded and said to myself, "For the moment."

Just a joke—but something sparked between us. She was beautiful, yes—but also warm, real, present. The kind of beauty that doesn't perform. The kind that just is.

We weren't a couple yet. But something had already begun.

Our first real time together—our first date—was at a Chris Tucker concert. Not in the audience—backstage. Chris was onstage doing what only he could do, setting the place on fire with laughter.

And Lynette was beside me—black jeans, black boots, a red top with a dark brown fur collar. Her shoulder-length hair falling just right. She looked incredible.

And that's when I kissed her. Our first kiss. With Chris cracking up the crowd a few feet away, and the building vibrating with joy.

As I shifted slightly—just turning the way people do when something shifts inside them—I noticed him. Richard Pryor, sitting quietly in his wheelchair, already looking at us.

He didn't say a word. Just watched. And right then, a slow grin began to rise across his face.

That grin felt like a kind of blessing. Like he saw something real in that moment, and it made him smile. That was the kiss. The kind that lives with you. The kind that returns to you years later like a melody you forgot you knew—soft, vivid, and exactly right.

The Day I Married LaNette

I woke up that morning with sunlight pouring through the window. It was the first of December, 1996—a Sunday—and though the light was bright, I could tell from the way the sunlight shined through the atmosphere that it was a little crisp outside. The kind of cold you don't feel until you step out, but you know it's there.

I had coffee and moved around my apartment slowly, doing little things here and there before heading out for what I'd been waiting for my whole life. My friend Chris was coming to pick me up, and we were riding down to Long Beach together. When he called from his vehicle and said he had arrived, I told him I'd be right out.

I was wearing something special that day—a French Edwardian suit made of wool crepe. It had a long morning coat, ruffled cuffs, and a high-neck shirt tied at the collar, with ruffles from the collar to the first button of the coat. A soft, long bow was part of the shirt's design. It felt like I'd stepped out of time and into a love story.

Chris and I got on the 405 freeway, then to the 710 that led us straight into downtown Long Beach. We arrived early—maybe around 11—and wandered into the Sheraton Hotel to kill some time. We sat quietly at the bar, drinking juice or water, just waiting. The bartender didn't charge us, probably sensing the occasion. Eventually, it was time. We left the hotel and headed to La Opera, a charming Italian restaurant on Pine Avenue. Chris, being Chris, walked right through the door I opened—for myself. That made me laugh. The main floor was already decorated for the holidays, but our ceremony was taking place downstairs, in the lower level, where the air felt warmer, softer, more intimate.

When we stepped in, guests were already arriving. People admired my outfit, helped straighten my bowtie, and smiled in that knowing way you do at weddings—like everyone's holding a little bit of joy just under the surface.

One of my friends walked up to me and said, "Antwone's getting married!" I replied, "You guys got married!" I was nervous.

Then the music started. LaNette came down the aisle on her father's arm, and I saw her in her wedding dress for the first time. She was stunning. All I could do was smile and hold my breath as she got closer. Chris Tucker stood beside me as my best man, trying to behave—but of course, when the time came to hand over the ring, he started playing games, pretending not to have it. Cracking a joke that had everyone laughing. That's Chris. Even in serious moments, he brings joy.

Reverend Buggs was the officiant. When we got to the moment, instead of saying, "You may now kiss the bride," he looked at me and said, "Antwone..."

I paused. Then he smiled and said, "Legally, now. You may kiss the bride."

The room burst into laughter.

After the ceremony, we all moved into the adjoining room for dinner. It was small, warm, and filled with love. LaNette and I are both vegetarians, so the entire meal was vegetarian, and everything was delicious. The cake came from Hanson's Bakery in L.A., a famed spot known for getting things just right—and they did.

Then came the first dance. Earlier that year, LaNette had signed us up for tango lessons at a senior center in Lakewood. Every week, we'd go down and be taught by a very nice older instructor. I can't remember if we actually danced a tango that night, but we danced.

Our song was Nat King Cole's "L-O-V-E."

"L is for the way you look at me...
O is for the only one I see...
V is very, very extraordinary...
E is even more than anyone that you adore..."

We held each other and moved to the music. Somewhere in the middle of the dance, her father executed the classic move and cut in. Another smile. Another moment.

At the end of the night, we stepped outside to leave. I thought Chris had promised to drive us to our hotel—but he'd arranged for a surprise. Waiting at the curb was a limousine. Instead of going straight to the hotel, the driver turned toward the ocean. We rode out to Malibu, driving in silence and laughter, down Pacific Coast Highway as the sun disappeared behind the hills. It was dark by the time we reached El Matador State Beach, the water, and quiet.

That was the first day. The first day of a journey that has now lasted thirty years. Still in love.

Once You're a Father

When LaNette first told me she thought she was pregnant, something inside me began to stir. I don't know how to explain it exactly—I just knew I wanted to care for someone from the very beginning. A baby. A child to love. I wasn't trying to fix my past or prove anything. I just knew, without question, that I wanted to be a father.

And when it happened—when I became one—I didn't feel burdened or overwhelmed. It wasn't about responsibility in the usual sense. It was joy. It was purpose. I realized: This is my life now. These children didn't ask to be here. They had no responsibility for their existence. That was on me. And I took pride in that.

I was in the delivery room when both of my daughters were born. I'll never forget it. When Azure was delivered, the doctor guided me—literally guided me—to help bring her into the world. I was the first person to ever touch her. I held her head in my hands as it crowned, and then I gently helped guide her body into the world. That feeling—it was like nothing I had ever known. I was terrified in a way I can't fully describe, but I also knew: I can do this.

With Indigo, I was the third person to ever touch her, but I was the first to comb and braid her hair. That meant something to me—something quiet but deep.

It started with what I could give them—education, housing, safety. Though I didn't think of it in those terms at the time, I just knew I wanted them to grow up in a community where they could see themselves. Where they could look around and know that success was not a fantasy, but a living, breathing reality.

So I bought a home in the Ladera Heights community in Los Angeles—at the time, the wealthiest Black community in America. That wasn't what I was aiming for in name or status, but it was the best I could do for them. In a way, it reminded me of Glenville. This was a neighborhood where, when people came home, they were financiers, architects, doctors, engineers, professors, filmmakers. You could walk down the street and know your neighbors had built something with their lives—and they looked like you. That meant something. That mattered.

But just like Glenville, there was a balance. Alongside the judges and engineers were pastors and small business owners. And there were a few people I recognized from another part of my life—former inmates I had known during my time as a federal correctional officer. Some had become residents of Ladera Heights, and some were simply returning home—back to the neighborhood they had lived in before incarceration. They were part of the same streets, the same rhythm of the community. That mix, that range of humanity, reminded me that success and struggle often live side by side. And that everyone—no matter where they started, or where life had taken them—deserves the chance to live in peace and dignity.

Some of those men were even part of our backyard gatherings. They weren't invited as anything other than neighbors. They came not as what they had once been, but as who they were now—fathers, husbands, homeowners, just people.

You could look across the yard and see a former inmate standing between a deputy district attorney and a judge—and you wouldn't know who was who. They carried the same dignity. That was the beauty of it. Everyone belonged. Everyone stood proud. And I was proud, too—of the life we were all part of in that moment.

We had birthday parties for the kids in the backyard, each cake decorated with their favorite characters—Barney, Superman, Batman. But it wasn't just birthdays. We held other celebrations too—cookouts, gatherings, just reasons to come together. There were always children running around, and we made sure there were people present to keep an eye on them. That mattered to me. Friends, neighbors, jazz bands playing, comedians dropping in. Lawyers, doctors, architects, judges—successful Black people, filling our yard with laughter and pride. I wanted them to see all of that. I wanted them to know their father was respected. That they were surrounded by possibility.

Whenever we hosted something—birthday parties or otherwise—I'd hang a colorful banner across the back wall of the yard. It read: The Function at the Fish House. That was my nickname—Fish. My childhood friends from Parkwood Elementary gave it to me, and I grew to love it. So when people came over, that banner let them know: this wasn't just a party—it was The Function at the Fish House. Ours. Joyful. Full of life.

And we eventually moved from that house in Ladera. We had lived there for many, many years. I remember turning back to look at it one last time—as if it were a living thing. The house was only three years old when we bought it. And when we left, I thought to myself: That house had only ever known love. The sound of laughter. The footsteps of children. The music of a Black family thriving. That meant something to me. Still does.

I felt honored. Still do. Even now, when they look at me, I can tell they feel secure. They trust that things will be okay if I'm around. And no matter how old they get, I'll always be their father. I'll always be here to guide them, to love them, to help them feel safe and grounded.

I once made a documentary about a man named Leon Garr. He was 96 when I met him, and over 100 by the time we finished filming. He worked in construction, and I remember one day watching him help build a room onto his grandson's house—three generations working side by side. That day, Mr. Garr seemed upset. I asked what was wrong, and he said, "I have to talk to my son. I have to straighten him out." His son was 75 years old. And yet, he was still his son. Still looking to his father with respect.

I've never forgotten that. Being a father doesn't end—it shouldn't. It's a lifelong bond. And thank God it is, because where would I be without being a father?

I don't think I've done anything special. I've just done what I was guided to do. I love my children. I've always tried to keep them safe. I made sure they had an education, never went hungry, and always saw themselves as valuable, capable, and surrounded by people who looked like them and succeeded. It's not about bragging. It's not about proving anything. It's about love. I feel it every time I see them. Even now, as adults, I try to step back and let them make their own decisions. But I'm still here. I'll always be. Because once you're a father, you're a father. Forever.

I Fell in Love with Words

I'm dyslexic.
But I didn't know that when I was a child. I just knew I couldn't read like the other kids.

I sat in class with my friends—Janine, Michael—and watched them read out loud like it was nothing. Sentence after sentence. Smooth, confident. I didn't know what they were seeing on the page, but I knew it wasn't what I was seeing.

Michael couldn't read that well either. But even then, I still felt alone in it.

The school tried to help.
Every Friday, a man from Case Western Reserve came to work with me. I remember his kindness. On his last day, he gave me a gift—a big book of Peanuts cartoons. Maybe he thought it would be easier for me.
It was. But it didn't fix the problem.
And eventually, I stopped trying to fix it.
I told myself: I'll just read what I have to read.
Street signs. Bus numbers.
That's all I'll need to survive.

No one could've told me that I'd one day become a writer.

But the Navy changed that.

When I joined, I had to take a test. I froze when I heard the word. I knew what it meant: a pencil, a paper, a page full of words. But I passed. I got in. And the reading didn't stop there. As I rose in rank, I had to write evaluations—training reports, official memos. I worked hard on those, tried not to make mistakes. And one day, someone complimented my writing.

That changed everything.

I didn't expect pride to come from the one thing I feared most.

But it did.

That was the beginning.

Over time, I fell in love with words. Not just reading them—but writing them.

I still struggle. I still have to focus hard.

I've lost opportunities because of dyslexia—reading scripts on the spot, using teleprompters, even on stage where shyness adds another layer. But I've also gained a voice. A powerful one.

Maybe I wasn't meant to take every opportunity that passed me.

Maybe the ones I did take—the ones I made—were the right ones.

I still read slowly.

But I write deeply.

And when I became a father, reading became something else entirely.

My wife is a big reader, and our kids grew up surrounded by books. We didn't get babysitters—we had date nights at the bookstore and brought the kids along. We bought so many children's books the shelves overflowed.

My wife told me I should read to them at bedtime. I tried—but I stumbled. The words wouldn't always make sense on the first pass, and my eyes would trip over the letters. So I made a decision: I would memorize their books.

I'd close the bedroom door behind me, sit on the edge of their bed, and recite the stories by heart. I acted them out, gave the characters voices. One of their favorites was Pizza Pat—I made a whole performance out of it. They loved it.

One night, my wife opened the door and realized I wasn't reading—I had memorized all the books. She said, "You have to read to them." So I asked my daughters, "Do you want Mommy to read instead?"

They said no.

They liked the way I read.

In time, the boy who couldn't read well enough to keep up with his classmates… became a writer the world knows by name.

They didn't care that I stumbled.

They didn't flinch when I paused or hesitated.

They just watched me. Listened. Loved me.

They understood what I couldn't say—Daddy's doing his best.

And in their quiet way, they gave me back something I didn't even know I needed.

Grace.

Tyrone

I had a bully growing up—well, I had a couple.
The first one found me on the playground at Parkwood Elementary, where I went to school at the time. He would wait for me to show up, then start a fight to show his buddies how he could push me around. Sometimes I ran from him. Sometimes he caught me. And when he did, I had to fight him—fights I don't ever remember winning. After school, he'd chase me down Parkwood Drive toward Drexel, where I lived. But he never followed me past a certain point—everybody knew a lot of knuckle sandwiches got ordered at that end of Parkwood, and I was real cool with all the servers. I couldn't wait to get him one of those, mouthwatering Sandwiches.

At the end of the school day, he'd run after me, and I'd take off fast—then slow down once I hit my area, turn back with a smug-ass look, and yell, "Come on—bring your ass down here!" He never would. At some point, I thought, he's not as dumb as I hoped.

But that was our routine for a while. He'd catch me again—usually on the playground—and we'd fight. It was exhausting.

One day he blackened my right eye. I put up a good fight. But that didn't worry me the most. What worried me was the thought of walking into the foster home with that black eye. Even an injury could be twisted into being my fault. I knew I'd be expected to explain it. To Valencia and Dwight—I could come up with a story for them. Something like, "You should see him! I tore him up." But the grown-ups were a different story.

So I went into the freezer, found a bag of frozen peas, and pressed it to my eye, hoping the swelling would go down before dinnertime. That didn't work—I had to face the music.

Funny thing, there was no music. Nobody asked. I sat at the table with a full shiner, and not one person said a word. Plates clinked, forged knives scraped, and I could hear people gulping Kool-Aid—the sound of it slipping down their throats.

Everything felt loud in the silence.

It was surreal, like a scene from *The Twilight Zone*—me sitting there, swollen and bruised, while everyone acted like everything was normal. As if my right eye wasn't nearly swollen shut.

I can't remember that bully's real name—but let's call him Tyrone. He was a thorn in the side of what I still remember as a beautiful neighborhood. A great place to grow up. And yet—he was part of it too.

Years later, I was back in Cleveland, filming. The catering trucks were feeding the neighborhood too, and people showed up—kids, elders, folks from every direction. The crew and the community really connected. There was a warmth to it. Then I felt someone behind me.

"Hey, man," the voice said.

I turned around—and it was Tyrone.

At first, I couldn't quite place him. But something about him—his face, his eyes—told me he hadn't played the cards life dealt him very well. He looked like he drank more than occasionally—maybe way too much. Like he'd been carrying a heavy load for years.

The weight of the old, once-powerful industrial metropolis—home of Superman—that made it possible to build lives and families, vanished—let him down I thought.

Life had been hard on him. I could see that.

He said, "I bet you don't like me, huh?"

I couldn't remember exactly why I shouldn't. But I knew. He was that kid. That bully.

"We were just kids, man," I said.

He smiled—but it looked unnatural, like it had been so long since he had a reason to. He was out of practice. And I felt a wave of sadness wash over me for him.

Then I asked, "Did you eat?"

"No," he said—eager at just the idea that he could have a meal with us. He got in line. And while he waited, I stood there watching him—up in line with the rest of the community. I wanted to help him. But what could I do?

I reached into my pocket and pulled out a $100 bill. When he came back to say goodbye, I handed it to him and said, "Don't tell anybody I gave that to you."

He nodded with that same smile. Took it. He looked like he needed it.

I told him to come back the next day.

He never did.

I never saw him again—but I still think of him.

Not for bullying me.

But for the weight he seemed to carry.

Hong Kong

I was stationed aboard the USS Cleveland (LPD-7) when we entered Victoria Harbor—Hong Kong Island to the south, Kowloon to the north. The ship was too large to dock, so we anchored out, surrounded by junk boats zigzagging across the water. We used them as water taxis, ferrying us to and from shore for liberty call.

Hong Kong was still a British colony then, a place I'd visited several times before. Crowded, electric, alive with movement—cars honking, neon signs buzzing, street vendors calling out in Cantonese. I knew a part of the city where I could find good food, familiar alleys, and shopkeepers who smiled when they saw me.

On that visit, I had my first taste of whisky—inside a place called the Far East Trader. It was one of those big, British-feeling buildings where sailors could shop duty-free, grab a bite, or sit at the bar. The whisky burned like fire. Didn't even make it past my tongue before I spit it out. My shipmates laughed, nearly doubled over. I couldn't understand how they were enjoying something so harsh.

Later, a few of us took off into the city. We walked through crowded streets, past towering apartment blocks with laundry strung between windows like flags. The air smelled like diesel, saltwater, and roasted meat.

In one shop window, I noticed seven or eight whole roasted ducks hanging by the neck—skin lacquered deep mahogany, glistening under heat lamps. Inside, a man in a white apron worked a cleaver across a chopping block, the sound sharp and steady. The aroma was rich—sweet, smoky, and savory all at once.

We wandered through those side streets until we found a park tucked between high-rises. Some local Chinese guys—around our age—were playing basketball. We stood off to the side for a while, just watching.

Then, without a word, one of them threw the ball toward us. Bobby caught it. And just like that, we understood—we were in the game. We just started playing. Five on five.

We were speaking English to each other. They were speaking Chinese to each other.

Then, somewhere in the middle of the game, something changed. They started speaking English—to each other, and to us—and the game opened up even more.

It felt almost magical. One of those moments you don't forget.

We felt welcome—and at home, in a sense.

Walking back, a shopkeeper caught my eye.

"Where have you been?" she asked.

I stared, unsure. Then she smiled.

"You were here two years ago."

Out of all the faces in Hong Kong, she remembered my face. I couldn't believe it.

Later, near a department store district, we saw something strange—a regular-sized Black man riding on a tall man's shoulders, weaving through the crowd. As they got closer, we realized it was El DeBarge from the DeBarge singing family. He was popular at the time, and we lit up.

"Hey, man!" we called out.
He looked surprised. "What are you guys doing here?"

The way he said it, you'd think we were old neighbors from back home. Like he couldn't believe we were standing there—just like we couldn't believe he was. El's maybe 5′9″ tops, but up on that man's shoulders, he looked ten feet tall. And the guy carrying him? He just stared straight ahead—stone-faced, eyes forward, like a camel trying to disappear. It was almost like he was thinking, "Good thing I'm all the way out here in Hong Kong. Ain't nobody I know gonna see me like this."

Then we walked up—and you could see it hit him: Oh my God.

"We're in the Navy. What are you doing here?" we said.
"I'm doing a concert," El replied.

I was hoping he'd invite us. He didn't. But the whole moment stayed with me—strange, funny, and completely unexpected. The kind of thing you just don't forget.

It was the smells. The steam rising from street stalls. The shine of duck skin in a shop window. The laughter on the court. The surprise of being remembered. The way the harbor shimmered at night, full of sound and wonder. I had found myself halfway across the world—and someone there knew my face.

Getting Out

I never imagined I'd work in a prison. But there I was—at FCI Terminal Island, locking cells, closing shackles, clicking cuffs.

Early on, most inmates were white-collar—guys who looked like they belonged at country clubs. But after the war on drugs kicked in, that changed. We started getting people from everywhere. Some were just lost. Others were truly dangerous.

What struck me wasn't how different they were—but how familiar they seemed. Until you listened longer. They were risk-takers. They rolled the dice—and they lost.

Even before the headaches came, I felt it—a heaviness. Something about locking a man in a cell or chaining him to a bed never sat right with me. Some officers handled it fine. I wasn't one of them.

I looked for the best in people, even when the job told me not to. And I worried that one day I'd miss something—and pay for it.

There were days when thick fog—parole dust, the inmates called it—rolled in from the bay. We'd be sent outside the fence line, out onto the slippery rocks between the water and the tall, high-voltage fence and razor wire.

Shotguns in hand. Waiting for hours, engulfed by gray. And I'd think: What the hell am I doing here? This can't be my life.

Once, I shackled an elderly inmate to a hospital bed after his surgery. The nurse was furious—she thought it was cruel. But she didn't know what I knew: he was dangerous. He had nothing to lose. And it was my job to protect her, and other hospital staff from him.

Eventually the stress got loud. Headaches before every shift. I went to the hospital, and the doctor said, You should find another job. Said stress like that could break a person.

So I left.

No plan. Just a rumor that Sony Pictures Studios was hiring security guards. Other officers joked and laughed at the idea—called it a step back.

As I walked out, a lieutenant asked where I was going. I said, I resigned. Feels like I'm getting out of prison.

He laughed—but his eyes said he wished he could do the same.

Some people stay in places that are killing them.

I stepped out on faith.

And what I found was that I had something more to give. I found my voice.

And it led me to the life I have now.

Todd

I met Todd Black through a mutual friend named Chris Smith, not long after the L.A. riots. I'd heard there was a free screenwriting class being held at a church in South Central called Bethel AME. So I went down there.
When I walked into the room, there was just one man sitting there—Chris Smith. He was waiting for anyone who wanted to learn how to write a screenplay to walk through the door. And there I stood.

I told him I'd heard about the class and wanted to learn.

He asked, "What do you want to write a screenplay about?"

I said, "My life."

So I told him my story the best way I could.

He stopped me in the middle of it and said, "You have a fascinating story. I have a friend who's a producer—his name is Todd Black. I'd like you to tell him what you're telling me."

I said, "But I'm not finished."

And Chris said, "That's alright."

Arrangements were made, and the day came. I went out to Todd's office in Brentwood. I remember walking in and sitting down by the window. Across the wide street, there was a school. I could hear the faint, joyful sound of children playing—a sound I'd known since my childhood in Glenville.

Todd sat down across from me and said, "Okay, Chris told me you have a great story. Want to tell it to me?"

As I spoke, I could feel that he was connecting—understanding that I was on an interesting journey.

I told him I had shared my story with a couple of other producers, but none of them would agree to let me write it.

They said I wasn't a screenwriter, that I didn't have enough experience. They'd hire a writer to tell the story, and if things worked out, I'd be paid for the life rights.

But when I told Todd I wanted to write it, he didn't hesitate.

He said, "Who else would write it?"

He told me he was negotiating a producing deal at 20th Century Fox, and once it was finalized, he'd reach out and let me know.

In the meantime, I had been writing by hand. Eventually, he read what I'd written. He told me he thought I had real writing talent—but I needed to learn how to write a screenplay. And he said he'd teach me.

He optioned my story, and that's when I started writing for real.

It was rough. Looking back at those early pages, I'm not sure I would've had the stamina—or the patience—to stick with me.

But Todd did.

He hung in there.

I wrote forty-one drafts of the screenplay before he sold it—and even more in development.

But he was constant through all of it. Every draft. Every rewrite. Todd was right there.

I remember once, after reading something I'd written, he said, "This is the most uninspired writing I've ever read. Go write something better."

He believed I could do better—and eventually, I started believing it too. I started introducing myself as a writer.

One day, I was in my little apartment in Inglewood, California, when the phone rang. It was Todd.

He said, "I sold your screenplay to 20th Century Fox. Go down to News Corp, bring your ID, and pick up your check."

So I did. And it was more money than I'd ever seen.

It wasn't all the money in the world—but for the first time, I felt the security that a little breathing room can give you.

But Todd told me, "Now you've got to get a job—this money won't last forever. And keep writing. People will want to know if you're just a one-trick pony. So write something else. Keep going."

So I did.

I found a nine-to-five and kept writing. Even then, I could still hear Todd's voice in my head:

Keep writing. Keep going.

It's one thing to have a good idea for a movie—but can you write a screenplay good enough to sell? Good enough to make a living? It's a tough business, and the only way to get better is to keep at it.

Now, after more than thirty years of writing, I think I'm pretty good.

But I know I still have room to grow.

You get better by doing it again—and again.

Todd got me started in this business—and he's been my coach and cheerleader ever since.

He was there at my wedding when I married LaNette—he and his wife Ruth. He was one of the first people I called when Indigo was born, and again when Azure came along. He's been a true friend for over thirty years.

Whenever I visit his office, I notice the NAACP Image Awards on his shelf—recognition for the films he's produced that uplift Black people. He has more of those awards than some Black producers and directors.

There's no way to fully thank someone like Todd—for his guidance and friendship, for setting me on this incredible path, and for helping me discover a talent I didn't even know I had.

That gift has allowed me to provide for my family—and to use storytelling to help others along the way.

The truth is, if it weren't for Todd Black, no one would've ever heard my name.

And my life—everything I've built—would've turned out entirely different.

Enem

I was teaching grad students at the *UCLA School of Theatre, Film, and Television*, and I had written a play for them to perform as part of their graduation project. It was a beautiful piece, and the students brought it to life with heart and soul.

There was a student named Enem—a young South Korean woman studying set design. She'd done her undergrad in Charlotte, North Carolina, studying art and design before coming to UCLA. For this production, she was responsible for the entire set design, and she did a beautiful job. Thoughtful, gifted, and easy to work with—everything she touched, she elevated.

The production was so well received that they extended the run. On closing night, her father flew in from South Korea to see the show. I noticed him in the audience—dressed with care, sitting quietly, proud, excited, and reserved. You could tell he had come a long way for this moment.

At the end of the performance, the cast and everyone involved in the production—including myself—went up on stage to be introduced and acknowledged. But Enem didn't come up. I saw her in the audience with her back turned to the stage, pretending—or so it seemed—to be talking with a group of undergrad students. I was confused. This was her moment to shine. Her father had traveled across the world to witness her work and share in her recognition, just like everyone else in the room.

But I'd taught at UCLA long enough to have a sense of what might be at play—her hesitation.

Then I saw her father looking around, clearly confused. Everyone who had helped bring the play to life was standing in the light, being celebrated. But his daughter—the one whose vision had shaped the entire production—remained in the shadows.

I didn't know exactly why she didn't go up, but I had a feeling. Maybe she thought she didn't belong on that stage. Maybe it was because her work had been behind the scenes. Or maybe it was about race. I recognize that too. The cast was all… well. I've been in rooms like that before—where you've done the work, played your part, but still feel like an outsider.

Whatever the reason, it didn't sit right. And her father's face told me he didn't understand it either.

After the onstage celebration, as the crowd began to disperse, I walked over and called her to me. I asked her to introduce me to her father.

She told him I was her teacher. And where they're from, teachers are highly respected. I saw it in his face—he understood the moment was important.

I looked him in the eyes and told him the truth: that his daughter was a genius. That the production would not have succeeded without her talent and vision. That she had inspired everyone else to rise to the occasion.

He beamed and turned red with pride. His eyes welled up. And then he pulled her close.

Denzel

I heard from Todd—he told me Denzel Washington was interested in directing the screenplay I wrote about my life. At the time, it was still called *Finding Fish*, same as the title of the memoir, though the screenplay actually came first.

Todd arranged for me to meet Denzel at an Italian restaurant on Pico Boulevard in Los Angeles. I think it was called Preemie, a place where Hollywood people went to talk business over lunch or dinner. Nice food. I remember when I got there, Denzel was already seated. I walked over, and we greeted each other.

Meeting him in person wasn't what I expected. Even then, he was a huge star—he had presence. But the vibe wasn't like meeting a celebrity. It was like meeting a man who happened to be known. He was calm, grounded.

I had already seen him around the Sony Pictures lot, where I'd worked security. His office was there. I even knew his wife Pauletta's cousin, Rita Pearson—we were friends. I remember walking down the hallway one day after an earthquake and hearing him talking about it. He was loud enough that I could hear every word. That lot had stars coming and going every day. Denzel was one of them.

He'd wave to the guards—waved to me too—but I don't think he recognized me when I walked into that restaurant.

Over lunch, we talked about the script—what I'd written, what it meant to me. He told me a little about his life, too. I was surprised. People see someone like Denzel and think he must've had it easy, but he came from a family just like the rest of us. Siblings, responsibilities, difficult times, people to care for. The more he talked, the more I saw the man—not the image. Just Denzel.

At some point—maybe not that day, maybe a later lunch—I offered to pay. I saw him pull out his card, ready to take care of it, and I said something like, "Sometimes other people want to pay." He smiled and said, "Oh, alright." It wasn't about the money. It was about being peers. About him giving something big to me, and me getting the chance to do something small in return.

I remember I used some colorful language during our first conversation, the kind I picked up from years in the Navy and working as a federal prison guard. He looked at me and said, "You don't have to speak like that, because I'm here." He didn't think I normally talked like that, and there was no reason to change how I acted just for him. I was probably just nervous—I figured a lot was riding on that lunch. But his comment told me a lot.

At the end of our first lunch, he asked me plainly, "Do you want me to direct it?" I didn't know whether to say "Hell yes" or just nod. I don't remember exactly what I said, but whatever it was—it was yes. And that's how it began.

We worked together with Todd and the team at Fox Searchlight. While Denzel finished other films—including *Training Day* and *Out of Time*—he kept coming back to the script he'd decided should be called *Antwone Fisher*. He'd work on it, step away, then return.

And then one night, we got the green light.

I was nervous. But Todd and Denzel moved through it like they'd done it a hundred times before. I followed their lead.

We were set to film at 32nd Street Naval Station in San Diego, and in the Glenville neighborhood in Cleveland, where I grew up. But then 9/11 happened, and the Navy base went into lockdown. We weren't sure we'd get permission to shoot. Eventually, they cleared it.

Nobody had told me I was going to Cleveland. I was walking through the Westside Pavilion Mall in Los Angeles with LaNette when I got the call. It was Denzel.

"Where are you?" he asked.

"I'm at the mall on Pico," I said.

"Why aren't you in Cleveland?"

I told him I didn't know I was supposed to be there. He said, "Well, I'm leaving tomorrow. You can ride with me."

The next morning, he sent a car. It brought me to his house, where I waited.

Pauletta came out with their kids—John David, Olivia, Katia, and Malcolm—loaded them into an SUV, and drove them off to school.

Then Denzel and I rode to a private airfield and boarded a private jet to Cleveland. As the plane lifted, I remember looking out the window, watching the ground fall away beneath us.

We were headed back to where it all began.

Up in the air, it was just the two of us, the flight attendant—and of course, the pilot. Denzel reached into his bag, pulled out my screenplay, and started reading it out loud, acting out lines, going through it with full attention.

I just watched him, stunned. Maybe he knew I wasn't comfortable reading aloud. Or maybe he just wanted to give it that kind of care. Whatever it was, it meant a lot.

He cared. That was clear.

As we approached Cleveland, I looked out the port-side window and saw the Terminal Tower coming into view. Denzel stood and looked out too. "Is this Cleveland?!" he asked. I said, "Yeah. This is my hometown." And I felt this swell of emotion—like I was looking at my past, still standing, still holding on.

We filmed in Cleveland. I took him and Todd to the DuPont house where I grew up. Another family lived there, but they let us walk around. I showed them my hiding place, up high near the ceiling. It was so small I couldn't imagine myself ever being small enough to fit there. Only Dwight knew about it, and he never told a soul.

We walked down to the park where the metal sliding boards used to burn our legs in the summer. On the way down a little slope, Denzel suddenly stopped. I looked over and saw what he saw—a group of guys around a car, likely up to no good. They saw us, jumped in, and sped off. Denzel still had that street radar. He never lost it.

One day during a break from filming, I stepped outside and people in the neighborhood started asking for my autograph. I was signing a few when I heard a voice behind me—"Signing autographs?" It was Denzel. His tone was playful, but firm. Like, "Come on, man." I tried to explain, but I was half-smiling, half-serious—my mouth didn't know what to do. It was one of those moments where you're both caught and amused.

Later, after post-production, they screened the movie for me at Fox Studios, in what's known as the little theater. Watching it alone was overwhelming. I didn't even have words afterward. I stepped out and called Denzel. I told him I loved it. I thanked him.

And I meant it—I'll always mean it. I was under Denzel's umbrella of protection. That's a safe place to be in this business. He's helped me, championed me, and treated me like I mattered.

If I lived forever, I'd never be able to thank him enough for *Antwone Fisher*
and everything else.

The Sandman

At the federal prison where I worked, I was assigned to C-Unit that day. I had just finished making my rounds and was sitting behind the desk in the officer's station when a 23-year-old inmate walked over. The other inmates called him The Sandman.

Before he could speak, I asked, "Why do they call you The Sandman? That's a pretty cool name. Were you knocking people out on the street?"

He shook his head. "Nah, I got the name in here."

"Why's that?"

"If you haven't noticed, I sleep a lot," he said. "I try to sleep at least twelve to sixteen hours a day."

"That's a lot of hours," I said.

He nodded. "Yeah. I got forty-five years ahead of me here. I figure if I can sleep at least twelve hours a day, I can cut my sentence in half."

He said it with a straight face. No bitterness. Just math. Then he added, "Today, I hope to see my mom in my dreams."

I remember laughing a little when he said it. Not because it was funny—but because he meant it. And because it was the only way he could make sense of that much time at such a young age.

He was just twenty-one when he got caught at LAX. Profiled. They found sandwich bags of crack cocaine taped to his body under his clothes. Conspiracy. Trafficking. Crossing state lines. It all added up to a big number. By the time I met him, his life had already been shaped by prison walls, high electrified fences, and razor wire. Counting hours.

He'd come up with his own system for surviving it: sleep through as much as possible. Dream of home. Dreams of freedom.

There was something both absurd and deeply sad about it. But that was prison. The consequence for his crimes.

Working nights, I'd walk the tiers and hear men crying in their cells. Hardened men, broken by time. By the truth of how many years they'd lost. How many they still had to go.

I never called attention to it. I never said a word about it. But I heard it. I felt it too.

And it began to shape me.

That was part of the reality I came to know: how easily a young man's life could disappear behind steel bars and locked iron doors. And how the only way to survive it was to sleep your way through it.

    Trust me.

The Coat and the Chicken

After the Navy, I became a Federal Corrections Officer stationed at the prison on Terminal Island in California. One heavy rainy, rainy, rainy day, I stood inside C Unit cell house where I was assigned, watching the yard as raindrops streaked down the window in crooked lines, blurring the view like tears on glass.

Across the yard was the galley, and I could see inmates being searched as they exited—standard procedure.

Lieutenant Rosenberg was out there, patting down a tall Black inmate named Brown.

After the search, Brown headed toward my unit where he lived.

I kept my eyes on him. Something looked weird.

His trench coat moved strangely, like it was hiding something.

But Rosenberg had just frisked him, so I figured it must be nothing.

Brown stepped into the unit, saw me, and made a quick right turn.

"Hey, Brown," I said. "Come here." He froze. Then walked over.

"Let me see what you got under that coat."

He opened it—and there it was.

A whole roasted chicken hanging from a coat hanger, threaded clean through the cavity, swinging from the armpit of his coat.

I smiled.

Didn't say a word.

Just let him go.

See, I didn't let him get away with it exactly.

But I had to choose my battles.

I was locked inside that unit with 150 federal inmates. Drugs? I'd hammer them.

Weapons? Same.

Theft? Of course.

But a chicken?

I needed allies, so I had to give a little.

Some time later, Brown came to me and started talking about his case.

He told me he was part of a "family."

Not blood family—more like a crew. A tight group from Oakland who found each other in the world.

They ran drugs up and down the California coast, from L.A. to the Bay and back.

He told his stories like a stand-up comic—animated, wild, and almost charming in the way only a seasoned hustler could be.

Then one day, he brought me his paperwork—court transcripts, charges, reports.

I flipped through it, curious.

One page caught my eye.

A page and a half of names.

"Who are these people? Your crimees?"

He glanced over and grinned.

"Oh, no. No. Those are the deceased."

I stared at him.

"These are the people I'm convicted of killing," he said — like it was nothing. Like murder was just another day's work.

I'd been talking to him all day, forgetting for a spell where I was—and who he was. Then it hit me again—I was in a federal prison.

And I remembered what my job was.

Antwone Days

The Forest I Remember

There is a place I've never been, but I remember it like a home I once lived in.

A forest—not just any forest, but one that feels safe. The kind of calm that lets you sleep beneath the trees without fear. The kind of safe where the Earth isn't watching you—it's holding you.

The rustling of buckeyes, the scent of their leaves, the deep smell of rich, jet-black soil—all of it speaks in a voice older than language.

And the wind—the invisible wind. When I was a boy, I knew it was invisible because it's made of the spirits of the ancestors. Too frighteningly beautiful to behold in form, but always comforting. They caressed me—even in the storms.

As a metaphor, I've had to lean into the strong winds of life—just walk straight through, not around. Even then, I loved and appreciated their force—the ancestors training me to keep pushing forward.

The way sunlight cuts through the leaves, striking the soil like it's writing something sacred on the ground. The birds calling from somewhere far off—unseen, but rooting me on. I was never alone. That's almost everything to me.

Early on, I was being made ready for the stormy days ahead. I see now that the forest gave me everything I needed.

Even in the city, when I sit in a park, I feel it trying to reach me. The trucks, the cars, the voices—they blur into background noise.

But when the sun warms my skin, when the wind lifts just right, it reminds me that the ancestors are still with me—constantly keeping me close.

I feel like I'm receiving something—a download from the Source, and an upload from Mother Earth.

My wife calls days like that Antwone Days.

A Faithful Warner

Fear was with me from the beginning. As far back as I can remember, it followed me—a quiet shadow in the room, a tightening in the chest.

And when I was emancipated after high school—no family, no home, just the street under my shoes—the fear intensified. It was almost too much to bear. Sometimes I'd be walking and stop cold. I wouldn't like the way a street looked ahead of me—the shape of the shadows, the feel in the air—and I'd turn around and walk the other way. Just like that. No reason anyone else could see, but I felt it in my bones.

Nightfall was the hardest. The days felt short, but the nights were endless—long hours of dread, of not knowing where I could safely lay my head.

There were times when I could hardly think straight. My thoughts jumped like frogs across hot stones. I thought I might go crazy. Then one day, it came to me—not slowly, but like a flash:

Fear isn't the enemy. It's not a monster following close behind, not some spirit bent on haunting me.

It's a part of me. A friend. A faithful warner.

It took a while to understand that. To believe it. But once I did, something changed.

I could look ahead, reevaluate, and see that sometimes the street was fine. Sometimes the feeling was just a whisper—a signal telling me: Pay attention.

And I began to listen—not blindly obey, but consider what fear was trying to say.

I learned to hold the reins. I never saw fear the same again—not as a ghost, not as something to hide from, but as something that walks beside me.

It's served me well. I look back now, older, and I don't know if I would've come to that without the streets, without those long, fearful nights.

Fear was just as natural and just as important as joy, anger, or sorrow. A part of being human.

Endure

I don't feel lonely the way I used to. I'm surrounded by love now—my wife, my children. They've changed the way I carry the past.

When I was a boy, I hid my tears, my questions, my shame. I didn't know my father had been murdered. I didn't understand why my mother couldn't care for me. I got lost in the system—without answers.

I was taken in by people who were old enough to be my grandparents. And while they were abusive in ways that left a mark, they did put a roof over my head.

I was always searching for explanations. Back then, I wondered—Why me? Why this life? Why so hard? Why so alone?

But I don't live in that place anymore.

I've spent years reflecting, and I've told my story—not because I wanted pity, but because I discovered something that could enlighten others.

And somewhere along the way, my experiences became a powerful tool for others—some like me, some with challenges beyond what I've endured.

I stopped thinking of my childhood as something to be ashamed of. I stopped treating it like a scar I had to hide. I began to see it as something rich in life lessons. And from that endurance, something greater was born.

I don't use the word survival. That word makes it sound like I was only a victim. Like I barely made it. That's not how it feels to me. I endured—and there's a difference. I leaned into the pain. I gritted my teeth. I squinted my eyes and pushed through. Not around it. Through it.

It's the best way past difficulties—because then you don't have to look back in fear. You sliced through it. I didn't go around it. I cut through it. I kept going. That's what I did.

Right before I was emancipated from foster care—before homelessness—my social worker told me something I never forgot:

"Don't feel sorry for yourself, because it doesn't do any good."

I didn't like hearing it then. But later, out on the streets, it came back to me. That line sped up my understanding. I had to do something. I had to stop waiting for anything to change. Hopeless as it felt, I had to get started with my life. I had to keep going.

You can feel sorry for yourself. But you can't live there. You have to tuck it away and keep moving.

You may need to pull it out from time to time—to remind yourself why you're hurting, why you're fighting—

but don't carry it in your hands too long. It will weigh you down. Keep going. Even when it hurts—especially when it hurts—keep going.

That's not surviving. That's endurance.

Restoring the Color

I was talking with my wife LaNette the other day about the reflections I've been writing lately, and I told her something I had begun to notice.

As I begin to compose these pieces, the memory resurfaces not merely as a thought. It returns with emotion.

Sometimes it comes back with the very feeling that once lived inside the moment. Sometimes it is almost physical.

I don't remember when the fading began, and I didn't notice when it had so subtly taken hold. For a little while, writing brings back the feeling of being there again. But the truth is, most memories do not stay that way.

Over the years, the physical sensation lessens. Memories lose their vibrant hue. Details begin to fade, like the color in an old 1970s Super 8 film, or the way a photograph softens into sepia brown.

The colors drain away.

What once felt vivid and alive becomes something closer to a watercolor. Then, sometimes, only a shadow. Some memories are reduced to a pale outline. Some begin to feel as though I only dreamed them.

I told LaNette about one of those memories from my travels while serving in the Navy as a teenager and young man — a particular memory I have always loved to recall. There was a small island in the Mariana chain where I had gone ashore for a little while. The sand there was black — volcanic black — sparkling like granule-sized diamonds, and beneath my feet I could feel the low rumble of the volcano that had formed the island in the first place.

I climbed a small ridge and suddenly found myself looking down over a lagoon.

The water was so clear it almost did not seem real.

Where the black sand met the water's edge, the color was pale and bright. As it stretched outward, it deepened into that rich blue anyone who has spent time at sea knows well — the deep Pacific blue.

The Pacific has always been my favorite ocean.

Clouds drifted overhead, and every so often the sun broke through them in long shafts of light, touching the water in scattered places like a gift for me alone.

I remember standing there and telling myself:

You have to remember this.

But time does what time does.

Even the most beautiful moments can fade if you let them. They become softer. Dimmer. Almost like something you imagined instead of something you lived.

And that is when I realized something about writing these reflections.

Writing them down does not merely preserve the memory.

It restores the color — the sensations return.

The faded photograph begins to sharpen again. The pastel becomes living color.

And suddenly the moment is no longer drifting away.

It comes alive again.

With my back against that shrine, watching the lagoon and the light for hours in the stillness—safe, still, and completely lost in the beauty in front of me.

Skipping Across the Years

Sometimes I find myself sitting alone.
Not alone intentionally—just the way life sometimes leaves you when the noise quiets down.
I've always enjoyed being around people, or simply watching them. But I've also learned to appreciate these quiet times when no one is asking anything of me.
And when the room is still, I notice something happens.
I begin to drift.
Not to sleep, but into one of my many thoughts and reflections.
Some people might call it daydreaming, but it isn't that.
It's quieter than that. Peaceful. Still.
And suddenly I find myself standing at the shore of a lifetime of memories.
From there, my mind begins to move across the years the way a stone skips across water—touching here, touching there. A memory from one time, then another.
Sometimes challenging.
Sometimes lovely.
Life can be difficult.
But it can also be lovely.

And when your mind skips across those years, you can't always choose where it will land. One moment it may touch a hard place, the next something warm or beautiful. In that way, it's a little like watching a roulette wheel spin. You never know exactly where the ball will land, or which memory it will brush against.
But they are all yours.
Every one of them.
The difficult ones.
The lovely ones.
When I was younger, there were always people around. As a little boy, a teenager, a young man traveling and working and trying to succeed—there was always noise, responsibility, movement.
Something to do.
Somewhere to go.
Someone waiting.
Now life has given me a different kind of space.
My work, in many ways, is remembering. Writing. Looking back across the years and trying to understand what I see there.
I've been doing that for more than thirty years now.
And sitting here today, letting my mind skip across the water of my life, I realized something simple.

For most of my life I was running through it—moving forward, trying to survive, trying to build something.
But now it feels different.
Now I'm no longer running through my life.
Now I'm walking through my memories.
And standing there at the shore, as my mind skips across the water, I realized something else too.
I've had adventure. I've had love. And days I wish had lasted forever.
How fortunate it is to have the time to do that.
Life is so complex.
But if you ever find yourself sitting quietly with time behind you, you may begin to see something else as well.
A balance.
The hard places.
The beautiful ones.
And if you're lucky enough to reach a point where you can look back across the years and see them both, you may feel the same calm that I felt today.
Just standing at the shore...
quiet and alone,
watching the stones of memory
skip across the years.

Black Sand

While in the Navy and on a goodwill cruise—island-hopping across the Mariana chain of islands. The mission was simple: repair generators, paint buildings, stock libraries with books we'd brought aboard ship and spread goodwill, hopping from island to island.

We'd been at sea for over ninety days when they asked for volunteers to go ashore and help out on one of the islands—whatever was needed. A chance to get off the ship—that was all most of us needed to hear.

My group of Black friends and I volunteered. But when the selection list came out, not a single sailor from any ethnic group had been picked, only White sailors. Of course we noticed.

So we stayed aboard, anchored just off the coast, watching the boats carry the others to shore.

That evening, when the volunteers returned, they looked miserable—faces and arms covered in bites from mosquitoes, sandflies, or whatever else was swarming that island. Nobody was laughing. None felt lucky, it appeared.

The next day, a new island—another stop along the Marianas. This time, none of the white sailors volunteered. But the rest of us did. Black, Filipino, Hispanic sailors—we were the only ones who stepped forward. And so we were the ones who went ashore.

And from the moment we landed, it felt like this island had been waiting for us.

The sand was black—smooth, fine, glistening like raw sugar under the sun. I'd never seen black sand before. Even across the shore, where the beach narrowed, the sand met the water in the same soft, glittering way. It was beautiful. I couldn't stop staring at it.

There was a volcano on the island. Dormant, but alive. You couldn't hear it, but you could see it looming high above the sea—and you could feel it. Steady and low beneath your feet, like the ground was breathing just under the surface.

I hiked a winding trail through the jungle up a low mountain ridge. At the top, the air shifted—and there it was.

A single shrine. Japanese. Weathered, made of cement and rock, scarred by long-ago gunfire—likely from an American plane during World War II. It stood quiet, worn, and proud.

I sat with my back against it and looked out.

The lagoon stretched wide below me. Palm trees leaned over the black sand, casting long patches of shade across the narrow beach. It looked like a place someone could rest for hours and feel held.

So Many Stars

So many times out—way, way out—with the ship cutting quietly through wind and sea, I'd take an occasion to step outside the skin of the ship at midnight, one o'clock in the morning—maybe later. At first, I couldn't see anything. But my eyes would adjust... and settle into the darkness—into something quiet and vast.

Even on a moonless night, the ship held shadows—cast not by the moon, but by the stars alone.

I remember one night in particular. The moon was nowhere in the sky. Still, the stars lit the ship so clearly, it was as if the moon had quietly passed the torch and left the heavens glowing a deep indigo—almost purple. The stars took command. They were everywhere—spread in every direction. Some clustered like family, others spaced far apart like strangers. No fog, no city lights, no pollution. Just clean, clear air... and the shimmering stars above me.

That night, I sat and stayed with it until they all disappeared with the dawn. I thought to myself, *This is something most people will never experience.* And I felt privileged—truly privileged—to be a witness. To have those stars—ancient as time itself—cast my shadow.

Out on the Pacific Ocean, we turned south—Australia, New Zealand, Fiji, American Samoa, Tasmania, New Caledonia—and so many cities in between.

I remember one warm night, climbing up to the signal bridge at the front of the ship where the signalmen were working. That night, the view was perfect.

The stars were out—accompanied by the moon. One of the first-class signalmen approached me and said, "Hey, you see the Southern Cross?"

"No," I said.

He pointed up to the velvet sky, full of stars. "There," he said.

It took a moment—but then I saw it. Plain in the sky. The Southern Cross.

So clear and beautiful, nestled in the night. I couldn't believe I was seeing it with my own eyes.

Every night out to sea held some kind of beauty—whether in calm or storm—but those nights, when the sky turned velvet and the stars lit the water and the ship… those are the ones I'll never forget.

And I carry them with me. Grateful to have been there. Grateful to have seen it all.

Sasebo

While in the Navy, stationed at Fleet Activities Sasebo, Japan. I decided to live off base and found a small apartment in a quiet neighborhood called Akasaki-cho—tucked up along a narrow, shallow, rocky river that flowed just behind the four-unit flat.

Fresh air came in through the window of my little apartment. I'd sit nearby on a tatami mat—the whole floor covered in that tightly woven straw, giving off its earthy, familiar scent. Through the window, I could hear the water washing over the stones—soothing and hypnotizing. In the mornings, the voices of schoolchildren drifted past in their black-and-white uniforms and randoseru—sturdy leather backpacks filled with books, notebooks, and the occasional bento. Their bags bounced as they walked, and the blending of sights, sounds, and scents stirred something in me—sitting in that little apartment, far from my beginnings and the culture I knew. And yet, I was embracing it all.

It was cherry blossom season. The trees were in full bloom. As a boy at Parkwood Elementary School, we'd learned about the cherry blossoms of Japan—and now here

I was, walking beneath them on my way to work, like something out of a dream. A boyhood memory come to life.

Each morning, I passed shrines where people waited their turn to step inside. No noise. No rush. Just reverence. I'd rise around five, prepare myself, and head out—following the river to the main road that led to the base. I passed older locals out for exercise, but no one ever spoke or even looked at me. I was invisible—so I thought.

I imagine I must have been quite the curiosity, the subject of quiet discussion in the neighborhood—the young Black man who lives up the road.

So I focused on the sounds—the river, the wind—and the teakwood-scented air.

After work, I'd stop by a little coffee shop in town. It had a small loft with a few tables and a view of the bar below. Record albums lined the walls—thousands of them. The owner knew where every one was.

That's where I was introduced to the music of Selena Jones, Sonny Rollins, and other jazz greats. I'd sit for hours, sipping coffee, thinking about the places my travels had taken me—home, old friends, and the world of my youth I'd left behind. This place was my private hideaway.

One morning, out on my usual lonely walk to work, I approached an elderly couple and—without even meaning to—I blurted out, *Ohayou gozaimasu*—good morning. The words surprised me. I'd stunned even myself.

The next day, everyone I passed eagerly greeted me. *Ohayou gozaimasu.* Good morning.

They'd noticed me all along. I just hadn't known it. After that, the walk meant more. It made my day lighter.

At the coffee bar, I looked different from everyone else—but I was treated like a human being.

Sometimes I think about that. About how strangers in a foreign land offered a kindness I didn't always receive in my own country—kindness not filtered through difference.

One winter morning, during the holiday season, I opened my door to head to work. A basket of fruit was sitting on my doorstep. A gift from someone in the neighborhood. A simple gesture—but it made me feel welcome.

That was Sasebo. A place full of quiet magic and charm. It taught me something lasting—about community, and about the quiet, powerful grace of being seen and accepted.

School Boy Crush

I think I was in the first grade when I first started liking girls. Real girls. Not just the idea of them.

There was one girl—well—I don't remember her name, but I remember her dress. It was yellow. She sat a couple seats behind me, and she was so pretty I couldn't concentrate in class. Maybe it was the funny feeling I got in my chest when I thought of her being so near to me. That was new to me. I didn't understand it, but I liked it very much.

Second grade, same thing. Third grade—same. There was always some pretty girl who gave me butterflies, whether I said anything or not. And I usually didn't. I was too shy. I'd sit with my feelings like they were a secret only I was allowed to know and enjoy.

Then in 1970, I transferred from Oliver Wendell Holmes Elementary—which once served as Glenville High School—on East 105th, to Parkwood Elementary on Parkwood Drive, just two blocks from our new hundred-year-old house on Drexel Avenue. And the butterflies started all over again. New classroom, new faces—and some new girl who made me forget the last pretty girl at the top of my love list.

Interestingly enough, as close as we were in proximity during school hours, I often felt unnoticed. I put so much effort into being seen—being charming, being funny—all the things I thought it took to make myself attractive. But as far as I could tell, none of those girls ever noticed me.

That started to change around fifth grade, when I began growing this beautiful Afro. It was nice—round, fluffy, big. I kept a pocket-sized can of strawberry-scented Afro Sheen hair spray in my desk and slipped it into my pocket with my frequent restroom trips to pick, shape, and blast my fro with that glistening sheen.

It was pride and perfection. I'd come back to class smelling like a fresh cloud of strawberries, and I believed the girls noticed—and liked me for it. How could they not?

That Afro became my crown.

By junior high, the girls started noticing me. But I started noticing—Freda Smalley. She was just my type. A little slick around the edges, and confident. I became a boy on a mission.

Neither snow nor rain nor gloom of night could stop me from my appointed rounds through the neighborhood just to pass by the homes of the girls that gave me butterflies. Eventually, I took all others off my route and focused entirely on Freda's house—a white duplex on Parkwood Drive, where she lived upstairs with her family.

Her grandmother lived in the lower unit—details I gathered during my routine reconnaissance missions.

I was sprung.

One winter evening—7 p.m. maybe—it was dark out. I left the house just to see if I could catch a glimpse of her. Of course, no one was outside—in forty-degree weather, in three feet of snow. But I stood in front of her house anyway, hoping.

Then, suddenly—the drapes flew open. And there she was, staring right at me.

The next day at school, she asked, "What were you doing standing out in front of my house?"

I panicked. "I was on my way somewhere," I said. "Then I started feeling sick."

She smiled. I don't think she believed me.

Years later, after I had become "Antwone Fisher," I saw her again during a book tour stop in Cleveland. I was doing a signing at Joseph-Beth Booksellers—a well-lit, locally owned store in Shaker Square in Shaker Heights, just east of the city.

It wasn't small—not at all. It was part bookstore, part gift shop, with bright displays and shelves full of everything from bestsellers to scented candles, keepsakes, and art pieces. The kind of place you could wander through slowly, letting your eyes land on something you didn't need but had to have.

She came to the signing. Time had shaped her in its own way. She was still beautiful, but you could see that life had made her tough.

Out of the blue, she asked if I remembered that winter night when she caught me standing in the snow outside her house. I laughed and said, "Ain't nobody stand outside your house for no whole hour."

"I saw you out there in the cold, snow, and dark," she said. "Just standing still, looking at the house for at least twenty minutes." She told me she had been peeking through the curtains, trying to figure out what I was doing—finally pulling them open because she was worried I might be freezing.

Me? I acted with disbelief.

She paused, looked at me, and in that telepathic voice-language all Black folks know, said something that had us both cracking up. That laugh was the most real intimacy we ever shared.

Back then, I remember pairing her in my mind with those puppy-love songs sung by so many soul artists we grew up on. She never would have imagined me doing that. But for me, she was a bookmark in my life set to music—

tied to fleeting moments of innocence before the harder lessons of adulthood arrived.

Then she said something I'll never forget: "If you and I had been together, your life wouldn't have turned out this way."

She meant it sincerely.

A little later, I asked about her mother, and she told me her mother wanted to meet me. So I invited her mother and a friend of her mother's to have dinner with me that night at the Ritz-Carlton in downtown Cleveland, where I was staying.

Her mother was just as I remembered her—only older. She said she remembered me too, though I'm not sure she really did. I think maybe she wanted to remember me. Maybe because everyone around her was proud. I could tell it made her happy to see someone from the old neighborhood doing well. And it made me happy too—happy that her mother got to sit at that table with a friend and feel connected to someone who had become known.

That dinner wasn't just for me. It felt like a celebration that belonged to all of us.

But I'll always be that romantic boy who stood outside that house with a stomach filled with butterflies in three feet of snow—hoping to be noticed.

What You See Is What You Get

That was the name of the song—*What You See Is What You Get*—by The Dramatics, my all-time favorite soul group.

Their music was the soundtrack to my early crushes and daydreams. Songs like *You're the Best Thing in My Life, Hey You! Get Off My Mountain, Fell for You, Door to Your Heart*, and *Be My Girl* weren't just melodies—they were anthems for every girl I ever liked in the neighborhood. Ron Banks, L.J. Reynolds, Willie Ford, Larry Demps, Lenny Mayes... they were smooth, cool, soulful. Everything I wanted to be.

We used to trade albums with friends in the neighborhood. I remember giving Freda—yeah, that Freda—my copy of *Cut the Cake* by Average White Band for her *Drama V*. I'd been dying to hear it, and when I finally did, it felt like a breath of fresh air. Even with all the chaos around me, their music gave me peace.

At school, I worked in the AV department. One day, Mrs. Thomas handed me a note and some money and asked me to run to a local mom-and-pop record shop to pick up five new 45s. One of them was *Fell for You*, fresh on the radio. During lunch, I played it in the girls' gym while students danced. The record player was perched high in the bleachers, giving me a perfect view of the floor below. The song swept me up. It gave me just enough nerve to climb down and try to ask a girl to do a hand dance—a soft, close partner dance we used to do. I made it all the way into the crowd... but when I got near the girls, I froze. Chickened out. Turned back, pretending to fiddle with the record player like I had something to do. Still, the song played on—and so did that moment in my mind.

Years later I turned seventeen, graduated high school, aged out of foster care, and became homeless.

I was staying with my friend Michael Williams, who used to sneak me into his room at night until his mom found out. One day, we heard The Dramatics were coming to Peach's Record Store in Bedford Heights. We didn't have money, but we went anyway—just hoping to catch a glimpse.

I waited outside for what felt like forever. Finally, a limo pulled up, and out stepped L.J. Reynolds, Ron Banks, Larry Demps, and the others. I didn't have a dime or a copy of their new album *Shake It Well* for them to sign, but I got in line anyway. When I reached L.J., he looked at me and said, "Hey, brother, you coming to the concert?"

"Yeah!" I said.

But I told Michael I had to go. We scraped together enough for tickets. Then he said, "We should take girls."

That terrified me. I was shy. But I knew exactly who I wanted to ask: Freda. Back in the neighborhood, I went to her house. Her sister Mona was on the porch. I hung around until Freda came home. She looked at me and said, "What are you doing here?"

"I came to ask if you want to go to The Dramatics concert."

Mona jumped in, "I want to go!"

Freda shot back, "He asked me, not you."

And there I was... me—for the first time in my young life, with two of the prettiest girls in the neighborhood arguing about who was going to go on a date with me. I felt powerful—for a moment, like I really was "The Man," as a trembling warmth swept through me, equal parts nerves and thrill.

With Michael driving, his girlfriend beside him, and me and Freda in the back seat, we rolled through the rain in his old Ford LTD toward the show.

The Bar-Kays opened, then Tower of Power with Lenny Williams. And finally—The Dramatics. Nobody stayed seated. And for about five minutes, I forgot I was shy. We danced, shouted, swayed—it was electric.

When they began *Just Shopping*, I had to stop myself from turning to Freda and singing the opening lyric: "I'd like to make you queen of my castle, give you all the things your heart desires."

And *Fell for You*, live, with Freda beside me? Magic. That's the only word.

Afterward, I walked her to her porch while Michael waited in the car. When I got back in, he grinned. "Did you get a kiss?"

I hadn't. As shy and awkward as I was, it meant the world just to have her with me.

Years passed. I had become Antwone Fisher. One day, a woman who loved my memoir *Finding Fish* contacted me through my website. I had written about The Dramatics, and she happened to know L.J. Reynolds. She told him about me, and he invited me to a party where they were performing—at Maverick's Flats in L.A.

I went. As I parked, I could already hear the music from the street. Inside, they were mid-performance.

And in the middle of a song, L.J. Reynolds spotted me and said into the mic:

"That's Antwone Fisher. I know him anywhere."

It floored me.

After their set, I sat with the group—Ron Banks, L.J., Willie Ford—talking, laughing, taking pictures. Later, L.J. and Willie needed a ride to their hotel near LAX. I offered.

So there I was, behind the wheel—driving two of the men whose music had carried me through some of the hardest years of my life.

The hotel entrance was jammed. As we inched forward, L.J., clearly frustrated, got out and walked up to the valet. I heard him say:

"Do you know who's in that car? That's Antwone Fisher in that car."

And in that moment—I felt like somebody.

He was tired of waiting, and he thought enough of me to use my name to get things moving. It was funny—and incredible. Before parting, we exchanged phone numbers—and stayed in touch.

I think what it was about The Dramatics is that they had the words I didn't yet have. They were saying things I felt for girls—but in a way I was too young, too unsure, too shy to express on my own.

And beyond that, there was something else. When I listened to them, I felt hopeful. I couldn't always explain it. It wasn't anything you could point to exactly—but it was there. A feeling that something was possible.

Maybe it was the way they sounded together. When you saw them, they looked like a family—like brothers. And when they sang, it was tight, in perfect harmony. Strong. Grown.

A lot of groups had that—The Temptations, The Spinners, The Intruders—they all sounded like men. But with The Dramatics, it reached me in a different way.

I don't know exactly why.

It just did.

The Boy Inside the Man

When I was removed from the foster home and placed in the orphanage, it felt like a permanent change—like maybe this was my chance to start over. I don't know if I had the words for it then, but I think I hoped I could reinvent myself.

By that point, I had already begun writing down my feelings. I didn't share them. In fact, I used to tear the paper into pieces and toss each one into a different trash can so no one could ever read what I'd written. But there was something about writing—just getting it out—that gave me relief. Not just when I was hurting, but when I was happy too. It became the way I learned to express what I couldn't say out loud.

I wrote the poem *Who Will Cry for the Little Boy?* during that time. I must have been fourteen, maybe fifteen, and living at The Metzenbaum Children's Center. Years later, I included it in my memoir *Finding Fish*, and again in the film *Antwone Fisher*. It was also published as a standalone poetry collection by William Morrow. And now —here, beneath the buckeye trees.

One day, I received an email from a woman whose son had the entire poem tattooed down the right side of his back—every line. She even attached a photo. I remember staring at it, stunned. I couldn't understand why someone would go to such lengths. But to him, the poem meant the world. She said her son felt it told his story. That it gave voice to a pain he couldn't always explain.

Then she told me he had died by suicide.

Her son had found comfort in the poem—at least for a time. She wanted me to know how much it had meant to him. And even now, I can't forget that. It was the first time I truly understood the reach of my story. That it wasn't just mine. That it echoed in the lives of others.

Since then, many people have told me how the book, or the film, or the poem touched them. But that message from his mother—that was the first one that made me feel something deeper than honored or grateful. It made me feel… responsible. Not in a burdensome way, but in the sense that storytelling matters. Words matter. Telling the truth—your truth—matters.

That poem was born out of loneliness. But I've learned that loneliness isn't unique. It's shared. My story is just one of many. I just happen to be someone who lived to tell it.

And sometimes, telling it is what makes all the difference.

Who Will Cry for the Little Boy?

by Antwone Fisher

Who will cry for the little boy?
Lost and all alone.

Who will cry for the little boy?
Abandoned without his own? Who will cry for the little boy?

He cried himself to sleep.

Who will cry for the little boy?
He never had for keeps.

Who will cry for the little boy?
He walked the burning sand.

Who will cry for the little boy?
The boy inside the man.

Who will cry for the little boy?
Who knows well hurt and pain.

Who will cry for the little boy?

He died again and again.

Who will cry for the little boy?
A good boy he tried to be.

Who will cry for the little boy?
Who cries inside of me.

Janise Womick

I received a phone call this morning. My friend Janise had passed away.

We met when we were nine years old—at Parkwood Elementary School, in Ms. Profit's class, where we spent the fourth, fifth, and sixth grades together. The students were more than a class. We were a family. I couldn't wait to get to school every day just to be with them. They were the family I chose for myself when I didn't have one of my own. And Janise was one of the first members of that chosen family.

My most vivid memory of her when we were about nine years old happened one morning during breakfast cleanup duty. It was my job that week to collect the empty cartons—milk, cereal, orange juice—from each student's desk. When I got to Janise's, she was still sitting there, sucking the last of the orange juice through a straw in the little wedge-shaped container. It made this funny bubbling noise.

I was getting impatient, maybe even a little irritated, and I shook the tray I was carrying.

She shot me a look like I had just insulted her.

Then, without saying a word, she doubled down—sucked even harder on that juice box, determined to enjoy every last drop.

I walked away.

But I never forgot it.

That was Janise—quiet, steady, funny without trying to be. Completely herself.

She told me years later—when we were probably eleven—that a boy our age had walked up to their front door, rang the bell, and her father answered. He was a self-taught interior designer who worked for a company with clients all over northeastern Ohio.

When her father, James Womick, asked the boy what he wanted, the boy pulled out a plastic toy wedding ring, held it up, and said, "I'm here to ask your permission… to ask Janise for her hand in marriage."

Her father ran him off the porch and halfway up the block. Janise and I laughed about that for years.

My life took a turn when I was removed from my foster family, and we lost touch for a long time.

We reconnected when my film Antwone Fisher was released. Nearly all of my childhood friends came to the Cleveland premiere. After that, Janise and I stayed in touch. We'd text—simple check-ins.

Hey, old friend.

How are you doing today?

I loved hearing from her. I loved knowing she was still in the world.

Just last week was her birthday. She turned sixty-five. She told me how happy she was to have made it to that age.

I sent her a little celebration—emojis, a big birthday cake, a slice of cake, and a bouquet of balloons. When she opened the message, balloons floated across her phone screen and confetti rained down. Her niece, Porsche, told me she showed it off proudly.

It made her happy to be remembered.

By me.

Me—the one who became a name people know.

But I never felt famous to Janise. To her, I was just Antwone. Her friend from classroom 209.

That meant more.

She was the last of her family. And I know she felt lonely sometimes.

On Parkwood Drive, where their house once stood, there is nothing now. It has been demolished and cleared away, along with the traces of a beautiful family gone from this world.

   But I remember them.

   And I remember the home they once occupied.

Once, when I called to check in, I asked her what she was doing.
She said,
    Just sitting by the window... watching the rain.
And even now, sometimes—on a rainy day—
I can hear her voice again...
    Just sitting by the window... watching the rain.

Meeting Ilyasah

I was on a book tour when I met Ilyasah Shabazz—and it happened in a way I'll never forget.

I had been flown into Atlanta to attend a book expo, and the publisher had arranged for a female guide to stay with me throughout the day. Her reward was a signed copy of my book, which seemed like a good enough deal. She drove me to the event, and we were escorted into a room where other authors were waiting.

That's when I noticed Judge Greg Mathis chatting with a woman who looked familiar—but I couldn't quite place her. As my guide and I passed by, Judge Mathis looked at me, and the woman turned. She stepped forward, looked me up and down, and delivered three unforgettable words. I won't say what they were, but they were sharp, unexpected, and hilarious. I was so surprised I couldn't stop laughing. Judge Mathis nearly doubled over. But she just stood there, deadpan. It was the funniest, most unusual way I've ever met anyone. That woman was Ilyasah Shabazz, and she was at the expo to promote her book, *Growing Up X*.

Later that year, I was in New York to speak at a literary event—I believe it was the New York Women's Book Club—and I checked into the Hilton Hotel. The person at the front desk gave me a room on a floor where the ceiling was so low, I had to stoop to move around. The furniture looked like it had been hauled in from somewhere else. It was dark, narrow, and nothing like what you'd expect at a Hilton.

I called my wife LaNette, and then I called Ilyasah just to say hello. I mentioned the room, half-laughing about how strange it was. She said she'd call me back.

An hour later, someone knocked on my door. It was a concierge with a key to a new room. This one was stunning—more like a private condo than a hotel suite, with sleek fixtures, a stocked kitchen, and big windows.

I called Ilyasah and asked what she did to make this happen.

She said, casually, that she had called the hotel and told them exactly who I was—and that they needed to do better.

That's the kind of friend she is.

Not long after, she came to Los Angeles to promote her new book, one she had written about her father's childhood. We spoke and I invited her over to spend the evening at my home. She brought three young women—family, cousins I believe—and we had the most beautiful afternoon and evening in my backyard.

I had the food catered. We sat around a round picnic table under a big umbrella strung with festival lights that lit up when the sun went down. The night had a kind of radiance to it—not magical, but soulful. Like something rare and deeply felt. Soul music played softly—Marvin Gaye, Frankie Beverly, that timeless sound of another era. The music wove through the evening like a warm thread, holding it all together. There's something powerful about sharing what you have. That night wasn't just about hosting—it was about connecting. I found that joy in my own backyard. Whether the gathering was large or small, there's something about offering a space to others and watching them enjoy it. And in return, they offer themselves—their stories, their laughter, their presence. That's what I felt that night. It wasn't just about Ilyasah—it was about all of us. Family, food, music, and spirit.

After that evening, I no longer thought of her as Malcolm X's daughter or Betty Shabazz's daughter. She was just Ilyasah. A woman of her own. And someone we came to love.

The Homecoming

When *Antwone Fisher* premiered in Cleveland, it was more than a movie showing—it was a kind of homecoming. We flew in—me, my wife LaNette, and our two daughters, Azure and Indigo—and stayed at the Ritz-Carlton in downtown Cleveland, just a few blocks from the Ohio Theatre. For some reason, the reservation was under the name Ranger Smith—Ranger Smith, from the old *Yogi Bear* cartoon. I guess that was the studio's way of trying to keep things quiet. It still makes me smile to think of it. That theater had always looked grand to me from the outside—but I had never been inside until that night. The Ohio Theatre was even more beautiful than I could have imagined—full of marble, rich details, and the kind of old-world elegance you expect from a place built in another era. (It's one of the jewels of Cleveland's Playhouse Square District—the second-largest theater district in the country, after New York.)

I had invited everyone I could find from my old life: friends from the neighborhood, Mr. Hayward, the corner grocer, childhood buddies, long-lost relatives, city officials—even my old social workers. The city had joined in too, helping to make it a true celebration.

That morning, after the premiere, I opened *The Plain Dealer*—the very newspaper I'd delivered as a boy, pushing a shopping cart through snow-covered streets. And there was a grainy black-and-white photo of me with Azure, just two years old then, holding her in one arm and carrying a sandwich bag of her Cheerios in my other hand. We were stepping into the Ohio Theatre. That image is still fixed in my mind. It said everything: I had a family now, and I was walking into a life I could hardly have imagined as a boy.

The night of the premiere, the theater was packed. I didn't sit and watch the film—I'd already seen it many times—but everyone else did. After the screening, I stood onstage with the city council. Looking out across the audience, I saw faces from every corner of my past—except my foster family.

My social workers were there. My childhood friends, including Fat Kenny—who introduced himself to Denzel as "Fat Kenny," embracing the name I'd written in *Finding Fish*.

Some of my other childhood friends were there too. They would say things like, "I'm on page 63!"—tracking their journey through my story.

The city councilwoman presented me with the key to the community. The mayor gave me the key to the city.

They even proclaimed December 13th Antwone Fisher Day in Cleveland.

It was a wonderful night. For me, it was also a kind of closure. I had left Cleveland with little more than hope. To return this way—with dignity, with my family beside me—felt like a full circle had been drawn.

Sometime after the premiere, I had to return to Cleveland again for some follow-up connected to the film. Fox Searchlight Pictures—the studio that had produced *Antwone Fisher*—arranged for me to host a gathering with my friends at a local restaurant—a nice place—and again, I invited everyone I could. This time, it was more personal: friends from my old elementary school class—Jenise Womick, Michael Shields, Gary Spencer. We even got Mrs. Profit, our elementary school teacher, on the phone. My junior high school friend Darryl came too.

That evening, as I made my way around the restaurant greeting people, I noticed Darryl trailing behind me all night. At one point, he asked, "Why are you doing this?"

I turned, half-ready to say, Why do you keep asking me that? But something stopped me. I could hear in his voice that he really didn't understand.

"If I were you," he said, "I would never come back here."

I looked at him and said, "You guys were my friends. You were like family for me."

For a moment, I'd felt embarrassed—maybe I was doing something strange, pulling everyone back in again after the big premiere. But after I said that, something changed in his face. I can't explain exactly what it was—maybe understanding, maybe respect—but I wasn't embarrassed anymore. Later that night, Freda arrived late at the restaurant and apologized as she approached me.

"I'm sorry I'm late. My car's not working, so I had to wait for a ride tonight."

Then she added, "I tried to come to your movie premiere. I got there, but the doors were already closed—and I didn't have an invitation anyway."

"I couldn't find you. I tried," I told her.

I can only imagine how disappointing that must have felt. Then she looked at me and said softly, "I hadn't read a book since high school, but I read your book... Antwone, thank you."

And I understood. I think what she meant was this: that no matter how her life had turned out—and it hadn't turned out the way she once dreamed—there was now a book in the world where someone had remembered her, and remembered her kindly. Someone had told the world that she was beautiful. That she was somebody.

I asked her what was wrong with the car. "I need a battery," she said.

I thought for a second and said, "I can get you a battery, but I'm leaving tomorrow at three—we'll have to do it before then."

The next morning, she called and told me which gas station to meet her and her mother at. That morning was cold and snowy—about five inches already on the ground, and big wet flakes still falling. The wind was blowing just enough to keep the snow swirling in the air. It wasn't a blizzard, but the kind of snow that makes everything feel hushed and slow.

The limousine stopped at the gas station before taking me to the airport. I went inside—they had the battery ready. Freda and her mother were there, bundled against the cold, happy that she'd soon be back on the road again.

I bought the battery, and she kissed me on the cheek.

I was surprised—and the first person who came to mind was Michael Williams, who had once asked me if I'd gotten a kiss that night I had taken Freda to see The Dramatics. It made me smile.

After I got back into the limousine, I looked out the window, and while the men loaded the battery into Freda's mother's trunk, I saw Freda and her mother almost celebrating, happily together in a few inches of snow, the air alive with swirling flakes all around them.

And then it struck me—the story I had been writing in my heart since first meeting Freda at twelve had just quietly come to its end. I let my eyes rest on the two of them one last time as the limousine slowly pulled away from the station.

Then I turned toward the airport, bound for Los Angeles and the loving family I had made, waiting for my return.

Where Were You?!

Living in L.A., I was missing my sister Valencia and decided to call—just to check in. When I did, a child answered the phone—my foster brother's daughter, maybe six years old at the time.

She said, "Uncle Antwone, I can't sit on the sofa—my grandmother's always sleeping on it."

I paused.

Grandmother?

I knew Valencia's mother wasn't in the picture when we were growing up. Valencia, her brother Dwight, and I were all foster kids—raised apart from our families. Their mother had never been around.

So I asked the little girl to put Valencia on the phone. When she came to the line, I asked, "Who's she talking about?"

Valencia said, "That's my mother. She's staying with me until she gets on her feet."

I was stunned.

"She's staying with you? Where was she when you were in the foster home? When you and Dwight were being mistreated—where was she then?" I couldn't hide my anger. I was more outraged than they seemed to be.

Valencia stayed calm—but I could tell she was a little intimidated by how upset I was. Still, she stood her ground.

"She said, Dwight wants her to stay here. You'll have to talk to him."

I knew what that meant.

When they were younger, there was a time their mother wanted to see them. Dwight was excited. Valencia refused.

So I understood this wasn't really her choice—she was giving in to him now. But instead of saying all that, she just passed the buck.

"You'll have to talk to Dwight," she said.

The truth is, even though I wasn't their real brother, they both respected my point of view. They never said, "She's not your mother." They never said, "You're not our brother."

And I never thought of them as anything less than family.

There wasn't a formal agreement between the three of us that we would behave like siblings—natural siblings. It was an unspoken truth that, for all intents and purposes, we were. The hard part was—Dwight was in Lucasville State Penitentiary at the time. I couldn't just call him. So I let it go.

Two weeks later, I called again. The number had changed. Disconnected.

I figured she was mad at me—maybe hurt by what I'd said. So I didn't try again. I thought it best to wait until she called me.

Some time passed. I had written another book and returned to my hometown of Cleveland for a signing at Joseph-Beth Booksellers in Shaker Square. That's when a woman approached me—said she used to be with Dwight.

"This is his son," she said, standing beside a boy. Then she added, "He's been trying to contact you."

And then she said something that knocked the wind out of me:

"You know Valencia died, right?"

I didn't.

The moment she finished the last syllable of the word died, I felt like my heart jumped out of my chest. It was so sudden. So painful. I felt like I could've lost consciousness.

She explained: Valencia had felt sick while driving. She pulled over and climbed into the back seat. She slipped into a coma. They took her to the hospital. It was a brain aneurysm. She wasn't going to make it. So they let Dwight out of prison under guard to be with her. He stayed for a few hours. Then he made the decision no one should ever have to make—he gave permission to disconnect her from life support.

I was shattered.

But I still had to sign books. I had to do the Q&A. I smiled through the awful pain, made it through what I had to do there, climbed into the waiting limousine, and rode back to the hotel.

But I was crumbling inside.

By the time the elevator reached my floor and the doors opened, I let out a lusty yell—strong and unguarded, the kind of cry only a child can give. I barely made it to my room, too weak even to close the door. I stumbled inside, collapsed on the bed, and wept the way I had when I was a small boy—until I simply could not cry anymore.

Valencia's gone.

When I finally connected with Dwight, he didn't ask how I was.

He just shouted into the phone, "Where were you?! I had to do that all by myself!"

All I could say was, "I didn't know."

It was heartbreaking. And then we cried some more.

Misunderstood

He's an old friend—a white guy by the way who, in the Navy, led a small division of diverse sailors on a ship where I was stationed. You'd never have guessed he held any bigotry. It was easy to be his friend—he never gave off that vibe.

But after he retired and moved South, I began to notice a subtle change in how he talked—edging closer to things I never thought I'd hear from him, hints of a hardening, tendentious worldview. Eventually, he'd open with, "Black people hate white people." *What's this business?* I thought. That became his entry point into every talk he began on race.

Even after centuries of suffering, some feel Black people owe them a debt of love. Entitled—expecting a debt never owed. How strange it was to hear—surreal. I hesitate to use the word "racist" because it's so loaded, but that shift in him was undeniable. One day he said it again—not with malice, just belief. And it stunned me—because he seemed to feel the need to keep saying it, and here it was yet again.

Seems there's a worn-out toy box of old lies and bullshit. And some people still pull one out whenever they need to quiet their conscience. "Black people are lazy"—though we built the economies of the Western world working from sunup to sundown for hundreds of years. We're not lazy. We're exhausted.

"Watermelon"—the crop that lifted us economically after slavery, turned into a joke to humiliate us back into the tiny space they carved out for us over centuries.

"Black people hate white people." Gaslighting. White fatigue. The irony.

These aren't lies—they're projections. They hand us their guilt and demand we carry it. Here's the truth: they know what's been done. They know the lies. And deep down, they know this: if we had done to them what they've done to us, they would hate us. That's why they expect our hate—maybe even crave it—to justify the story they tell themselves.

But what they can't seem to grasp is this: we don't have that kind of hate in us. We can feel anger, we can protest, we can resist—but the kind of raw, soul-deep hatred that was visited on us? Is not in us.

They accuse us of hating, when what they fear is being hated. When Black people say Black Lives Matter, it isn't hatred spilling into the street. It's centuries of injury rising through the throat—the raw nerve of being told you are less than human and still choosing to speak.

Then comes the response: All lives matter. And suddenly we're back on the playground, mocked with the grown-up version of "I'm rubber, you're glue." The message erased. The pain ignored. Some don't want to hear the truth—they already know it. Admitting it would cost too much.

Immigrants take the oath, learn our history—and somewhere between the lessons and the flag-waving, they absorb an unspoken rule: to be fully American, you must know where to place your disdain. And for many, that place is us—foundational Black people. Because what is America if not a place that, from the beginning, made Black life negotiable?

Forget the men and women we've buried. Forget the fear in the rearview mirror every time we see flashing lights. Forget that I have never left my house—not once—without factoring in my Blackness like a threat assessment. Forget it all. Because saying it out loud makes me the problem.

But no. This is not hate. This is self-preservation—an inherited caution. A love for my life so fierce I must guard it with all I have.

If Black people truly hated, this country would look very different—no prayer circles, no forgiveness, no mourning. Only fire. And yet we are still here.

Accept this or not—it doesn't change anything. This is the truth. And the truth never, ever changes.

The Hidden People

I've carried one question my whole life:
Who were we before our names were stolen—
our tongues, our place in the world?
Even as a boy, I felt something tugging inside me—
a buried voice begging to be remembered.
First came our true—but now mysterious—name.
Then the shuffle began:
Colored, Negro, Black, Afro-American, African American—
each reflecting the language of its era,
with a myriad of derogatory names in between.
But now, within the community, a new name is spoken:
Soulaans—
a name born not of classification, but of spirit.
All the others were merely a catalog of labels—
meant to define us, never to connect us.
Still, we remain—
not because it was allowed,
but because brilliance cannot be erased.

Father's Day

My daughter and I slipped out for ice cream,
just the two of us, laughing about nothing,
in a mostly white neighborhood.
The cashier—a young white guy—looked up,
and his face twisted before he could hide it.
A snarl flickered like muscle memory.
He tried to smooth it away,
but it kept returning.
I've seen it my whole life—
hate passed down like a rusted key
to a door that leads nowhere.
I'm glad I don't carry a useless hateful heart.
Still, I have to watch for it—
and warn my children.
My daughter, all grace, asked for pistachio.
He stared as if her voice stung his ears.
Later she whispered,
"Daddy, he looked disgusted."
I said,
"I know.
This is the hate I've tried to prepare you for."
He saw only skin—
and that was enough to make him snarl.
Skin that shines with a value they pretend not to see.

What he missed was Bantu blood—
blood that forged iron, built kingdoms,
spoke to God before there were churches.
The same Y-DNA as Ramses III,
carved forever in stone.
That line runs through me—
through my daughter—
ordering ice cream at his counter.

The Weight We Carry
My anger isn't new.
It holds every stereotype strapped to our backs:
Lazy—though this country was built by our enslaved
hands.
Dangerous—though the worst crimes were done against us.
Drug-ridden—though the drugs arrived by plane and
policy.
Guns we don't manufacture.
Loans we're denied.
Systems we never designed—
yet we're blamed for their wreckage.
Still, we endure.

Ancestral Grounding

I'm Bantu on both sides,
descended from people who never needed a book to find God.
They called the Creator Nzambi, Mulungu—
the breath in trees,
the rhythm of rain,
the wisdom of elders.
We aren't lost.
We were hidden—
shining anyway.

Purpose

That Father's Day reminded me:
my purpose isn't the scripts I write
or the praise I receive.
It's raising children who walk with dignity,
who spot hate and still choose grace.
Fatherhood never ends.
Even when they're grown,
I'll still be guiding, praying,
watching over them in quiet ways.
If the world won't love them rightly,
I'll love them harder.

That is purpose.
That is legacy.
Dragged into night,
we carried morning inside us.
We lost our names—
not our worth.
For us, knowing when not to speak,
when to let a man's poison pass without reply,
has always been a second heartbeat—
a survival rhythm passed down.
Now I see the wider world tasting that same caution for the first time,
calling it loss.
But it's the same rhythm of history I've carried all my life:
freedom isn't given,
it's practiced, defended,
spoken into being.
When I look at my children, I see the prophecy alive:
We were hidden—yes—
but we are still here.
And piece by piece,
we remember.

Our Souls Are Tired

These days, I see that same kind of warped projection in how some folks mock—one syllable, four letters—woke. When people mock the word, they think they've landed a sucker punch. But to anyone paying attention, it sounds less like insight and more like a bunch of goofy kids in the school yard, trying to sound studious and wise while repeating the same tired taunt. They don't realize they're announcing their own ignorance—loudly—like someone confidently mispronouncing a word they never bothered to look up, then laughing at everyone else for knowing what it means.

Woke simply means being aware—awake to history, to injustice, to the world as it really is. And the word itself isn't new. Black folks have been saying stay woke for generations—long before some tried to rewrite its meaning out of fear. Mocking that is like mocking someone for knowing how to read. It's not the insult they think it is; it's a mirror, exposing those who can't be awakened. Misusing "woke" is one thing. But opening a speech with it is another. That's not dialogue—it's a diatribe, stuck on woke. It becomes a dog whistle, cueing the crowd to lean in for a

rehearsed culture-war rant. The word itself is simple; what they attach to it is a script meant to stir bias, not insight.
This question comes to me in many different ways.
"What's wrong with Black people? There's every opportunity in this country—look at you, you did it."
That's how a white friend once put it to me.
"Why are we treated so badly in this country, and around the world?"
That's the question my Black friends ask, looking for my take.
Nobody likes us.
Nobody stands with us.
Hated even by sojourners and transient strangers.
Our souls are tired—of it.
Our bodies have been tired—because of it.
Drowning in fatigue—in it.
Hated without a cause.
How disappointing.
So many of us have died—been killed—from the time of our enslavement even till now.
Here's finally my answer.
Death toll alone does not define the scale or severity of what we've been through.
Structure does.
It involved systematic targeting of Black people.

Dehumanization as justification.
Deliberate policies of starvation, displacement, or execution.
And generations forced to endure unspeakable indignities—acts so cruel, their effects still echo through our bodies, families, and communities.
Global systems that enabled it—or ignored it.
In the courts, it's accepted that an abused child may grow up to be an abuser.
Judges and juries sometimes even grant leniency because of that past abuse.
But when it comes to Black people—abused for centuries—no such understanding is given.
Instead, the world pretends surprise—and fear for their own lives—when we turn that pain inward, when some of us show traits of abuse, or even harm each other.
But we never built a history of abusing others outside ourselves.
That destruction was done to us.
And now the same people who worked so hard to break us point with fake concern at the damage—
Blaming the broken instead of the breakers—
Accusing the victims instead of the villains.
We've been made into something we were not in the beginning.

We're taught by historians that more than twelve million Africans were forced into the transatlantic slave trade—captured, sold, and shipped as cargo across the ocean into chattel slavery.

Millions died along the way.

Of those who survived the Middle Passage, most were taken to the Caribbean and South America, with a smaller number brought into North America.

I didn't come into this world knowing any of this.

I learned it from books and classrooms, like everyone else.

And I've lived long enough to know that history doesn't always tell the whole story.

So I listen.

I study.

I remember.

And I stay alert.

There, chattel slavery took root—a system that was not just labor but ownership.

It was hereditary, passed from mother to child.

It meant a person could be owned.

Bought.

Sold.

Owned again.

Traded.

Given away.
Inherited.
Molested without consequence.
Beaten without consequence.
Mutilated without consequence.
Tortured without consequence.
Killed without consequence.
Stripped of name, of nation, of family.
Reduced to property, generation after generation—
causing the aftermath we live in.
That was chattel slavery.
The transatlantic slave trade spanned centuries—a slow,
methodical undoing of nations, families, and futures.
But of course, the forced movement of people wasn't just
Africans brought from across the ocean—it also included
Native Americans shipped to Caribbean plantations and
some returned, rebranded as Negroes.
But some things we didn't need historians to explain to us.
We knew them.
Our great-grandparents told our grandparents.
Our grandparents told our parents.
Our parents told us.
Through stories, warnings, prayers, and memories carried
from one generation to the next.
Colonial genocide in the Americas killed tens of millions.

But death is not the only measure of human catastrophe.
Intent, design, and silence matter.
If one system is built to erase a people—and does so in slow motion while the world watches—
then what do you call that?
The trade stretched across four hundred years of sanctioned suffering.
It devastated entire cultures and entire people.
When you add in the trauma passed down, the dehumanization written into laws and borders, and the systems built from that violence—
the suffering is incalculable.
It was a centuries-long genocide.
And we remember.
Remember the Devil's Punchbowl.
The massacres.
The lynchings.
The deliberate flooding of thriving Black towns.
Brutal, badge-backed abuse.
Human warehousing.
But because it happened over hundreds of years, it became normalized.
The duration doesn't reduce the violence.
It reveals a system so deeply accepted that atrocities became routine, even cavalier.

A genocide that lasts a few years is horrific.
A genocide that spans generation after generation becomes a way of life.
The trade wasn't a moment.
It was the making of a world and a destruction of a people.
We've been tired for centuries.
Our babies are born tired.
Souls already exhausted.
There are things I've learned to swallow.
Words, wounds, and the deep ache of knowing
I can't always speak my truth—
not without risking something.
Even among friends.
Even with people I care about.
Especially them.
Because in this world, a man like me—
a Black man—
doesn't always get to grieve out loud.
Doesn't get to question.
Doesn't get to feel rage without being called dangerous.
Doesn't get to feel empathy for the wrong dying child without being accused of betrayal.
There's a power some people hold
they don't even recognize.

The power to say what they feel without fear.
The power to send a hateful video
and still be seen as righteous.
And I feel that weight.
Because I live in a body
that has already been dehumanized for centuries.
I carry the memory—
of slavery, of lynchings,
of bodies sold and demoralized,
of babies torn from arms and breast,
of surgeries without anesthesia,
of ancestors whose suffering is too brutal to speak aloud—
with the knees of authority
pressed to the necks of Black men,
dying slowly
while the world watches.
I carry the knowledge
that in this society, even today,
my pain doesn't register the same.
And so I bite my tongue.
I nod.
I listen.
I let them speak their grief
while mine trembles behind my ribs.

But in my quiet,
I am remembering.
I am praying.
I am surviving.
And I will not forget
that my story is sacred, too.
I don't have to explain myself
to people who've never learned to listen.
Not when I carry something deeper than opinion—
I carry origin.
I descend from the same line
that birthed Ramses III.
My blood is older than borders,
older than languages,
older than hate.
It remembers.
It remembers
when the world was still waking up.
It remembers
the sound of Nile water against temple walls,
and the hum of ancestors
speaking through stars.
I am not rootless.
I am not accidental.
I am ancient.

So when someone disregards my humanity—
when they talk over my grief,
or send me messages filled with rage
and blind allegiance,
or carry the threat of false labels
in their back pocket—
I don't have to match their ignorance.
I can stand inside this reality.
Because not everyone can say:
I come from the beginning.
Not everyone can say:
My DNA traces back to the dawn.
But I can.
And I do.
And that is enough.

Who I Am

There was a time when I didn't know my mother or father's name.
Didn't know what part of the world my people came from.
Didn't have a story, a photograph, or a place to trace my beginning.
All I had was silence.
And questions.
But I've learned something since then—
Sometimes the silence isn't the end of the story.
Sometimes it's just the space you grow strong enough to fill.
What follows is not just about DNA or ancestry.
It's about finding out I was never empty.
I was full of history the whole time—
I just had to reach for it.

For all of my childhood, I didn't know where I came from.
I was a foster kid—
a boy without a family story,
without a last name that connected to anything
but paperwork at the child welfare office
in Cleveland, Ohio.

But life has a way of revealing what's yours—
even if it takes a while.

At age thirty-three, I found my family.
They told me everything they could,
and for the first time,
I knew I belonged to something.
I learned what they knew.
And then I kept going.

I searched deeper.
And what I found
went beyond anything I imagined.
Through DNA research, I discovered
that I descend from one of the oldest haplogroups on Earth
—E1B1A.
These were not just the ancestors they said we were—
the ones from the story we were handed.
These were people who stood at the beginning.
People who migrated, endured, survived.
People whose bloodlines walked this land
long before this civilization took shape—
long before anyone came along to rename it...
or to tell us where it all began.

I share a lineage with Pharaoh Ramesses III
of Egypt's Twentieth Dynasty.
I learned that my grandmother was born Emma Blount.
My great-grandmother was Ida Jolliff.
A document showed that my second great-grandfather,
Moses Fisher—born in 1840—
served in the Civil War at the age of twenty-three
as part of the Union Army's Colored Troops.
He fought to free his people—
Black people—from slavery in America.

What's wild is this:
I now know more about where I come from
than most people who grew up inside their families.
I had no story once.
But now I have volumes.

Now I have roots—
not only in the branches of recent generations,
but reaching all the way down
to the origin of man.

Our elders told of the ship *Providence*—
and others like her.

How it carried us out—
not too far, but far enough
we could not easily reach—
then brought us back.
A round trip.
With new names stitched to our skin.
Like the water...
and the time...
had washed away where we came from...
who we truly were.

But that's the oldest trick there is.
Isn't it.

Taken... hidden... renamed.
That's the story we Black people in America are left holding.
And so we ask—
Who are we?

And the voices rise back—
We are the ones who can't be erased.
For if you cut the root,
the whole tree will wither and die.

Ever, the answer drifts a little closer—
drifting ever to shore.

What Forgiveness Gave Me

They came from the heart of the Deep South—Laurel, Mississippi—where the brutal past still haunted the living.

Like so many families of the Great Migration, they brought those memories north to cities like Cleveland, where I would eventually come into their lives.

My foster parents were already in their later years when I arrived in their home. My foster father was born in 1908, and my foster mother in 1913. I was born much later.

Almost certainly, their own grandparents—who had lived through slavery itself—helped raise them. And in turn, my foster parents were shaped by that direct legacy of bondage and the aftermath that followed.

In other words, I was raised by those whose lives were molded by both those who had been enslaved and those who had survived its immediate legacy. And eventually, that legacy would shape me too.

What got passed down, for some, wasn't tenderness. It was survival.

And I want to be clear—this isn't reaching, it isn't imaginary, and it's not some distant theory.

Chattel slavery—its horrors beyond words—was only yesterday in the brief lifetime of this nation, and in its memory. My foster father's grandparents were born into it—suffering every aspect of slave plantation culture and the many forms of its evil consumption.

That's not ancient history; that's living memory, passed down through hands, through habits, through scars that have never disappeared.

For centuries, America's wealth was built on slavery. Cotton became the nation's leading export, and countries around the world depended on it. The global economy itself ran on the forced labor of Black chattel slaves in America.

The shadow of slavery lingers still, in the struggles and scars carried by Black families. The pain we live with—ineffable.

Some will deny this, say we should have "moved on," that what happened generations ago couldn't shape what we became.

I'm not here to convince them, nor am I asking for anything. This is simply how it happened, how it was handed down, how I lived it.

And to those of us who have inherited these scars—who sometimes wonder why the hurt still sits so close—this is why.

This is the story behind the silence and the reason certain wounds run so deep.

But make no mistake: the effects of chattel slavery are part of who we are as a people, whether that fact is accepted or not. To say otherwise is to attempt an erasure that cannot be done.

Its damage is still lived out in the families and communities of Black people today.

Some things don't just fade away. They settle into the bones of a family… a community… a people… and become a kind of norm—into the way love is given, or withheld.

And yet, after centuries of building the wealth of nations, Black people are still too often treated as if they are nothing, when in truth the world was built on their labor.

But of course—this is all very old news.

I didn't understand any of that as a child. I only felt the pain.

And not just physical pain—though I knew that too.

They called them whippings back then—a word that carried the dust of the plantation, the sting of the lash, the memory of slave masters and overseers driving it into flesh.

Years later, I interviewed an elder from Ruston, Louisiana, named Leon Garr, for a documentary I made about his life.

Born in 1914, less than fifty years after slavery, he told me about a whipping he witnessed as a young man.

His voice shook as he remembered it—the image still vivid in his mind:

"They forced the old Black man down over a log and held him there. Tore his clothes off like they was wild dogs. Then they took a belt and whipped him—takin' turns—for more than thirty minutes! A grown man! Like he was a child. And they TORE INTO 'EM! He kept begging, 'What did I do? What did I do?' over and over till his voice gave out. I knew he didn't have to do nothin'. He was scared near to death. I thought they was gonna kill him."

And with a grimace, almost like an exclamation point, he muttered:

"I seen that."

That memory never left him.

As for me?

Discipline—whatever name you put on it—it hurt.

And sure, the body forgets after a while.

But the memory doesn't.

That's what stays.

That's what hardens—memory turning to scar tissue, layer upon layer.

And that's what I had to work through to finally reach forgiveness.

Some of it was things that were said to me.

Words meant to cut.

And they did.

Words like:

"Don't nobody want you! And don't think I want you because you're here!"

As a child, you don't understand why anyone would say something like that to you.

You just carry it.

As a boy, I often felt cheated out of my foster father's love, though I never said it aloud.

Once, I told Mercy, his biological daughter, "He never talked to me," longing for the love I thought I was supposed to have.

She said, "He never talked to us either."

Only then did I start to see that love can take quieter forms.

His presence, the way he sometimes looked at me—that was his way of giving what he could.

Years later, Valencia reconnected me with one of my foster parents' older daughters—I'll call her TDB.

She mailed me a grainy black-and-white photograph of me at about four or five, sitting beside Dwight on the stoop of the DuPont house.

That same image was later cropped by the publisher to show only me, and used for the cover of my memoir, *Finding Fish*.

Tucked in with it was also a copy of my foster father's obituary.

When I opened it and read down to the "survived by" section, I saw my name listed—first after his biological children:

Antwone Fisher of Los Angeles.

Then came Valencia and Dwight.

After everything, I sat there staring at that line for a long moment.

I was more than stunned; I was shaken.

In my mind, I'd been convinced they never truly considered me family, not after the way I'd been treated.

But seeing my name listed there—right among their own children—made me pause.

It was like a small piece of truth I hadn't expected.

And maybe that was the moment the path to forgiveness quietly began.

Strong as a bull, with muscles to match, one of the last things I remember him saying to me came in that proud, weary yet unbroken Southern Mississippian Black male voice—a voice shaped by generations of denied dignity, yet still carrying the strength God gave him to endure.

His whole story was in that voice.

He said to me:

"Boy—he'd call me that—make a niiiiice young man outchaself."

And I answered, "Yes, sir"—the way young people were expected to address their elders.

Well… I hope I did.

And yet, even through all of that, I found myself sharing pieces of my past.

When I was in the Navy, I would talk about my childhood to some of the guys.

But I didn't share it the way I felt it.

I made it funny.

I made light of it.

I mocked my foster mother's voice, mimicked her sayings.

It was how I let myself express it—without letting it take me under.

Over the years, I learned I could shape the same memory different ways.

My wife LaNette once said:

"You could tell that same thing and have someone laughing, or tell it again and leave them in tears."

And I suppose that's the mark of someone who's had a lot of practice.

But also, someone who's been trying to carry a truth in a way that won't crush him.

One day I was talking with LaNette again about my foster parents.

But this time, I wasn't mocking them.

I was remembering how industrious they were.

My foster father ran his own lawn care service, with many clients on the west side of Cleveland where the "good-paying" white folks lived.

He even healed my eczema once with a salve he made himself from leaves and things of the earth.

The doctors had tried everything, but nothing worked—until his remedy cleared my skin.

The dermatologist asked what we had used, and my foster mother said simply that her husband had made something special.

But they never shared the formula.

When they prepared for the seasons, it was something to see.

Relatives sent food from Mississippi—frozen meat, peas, vegetables—all stored in the deep freezers around the house.

They knew how to survive without daily trips to the store, making and stretching what they had.

I told my wife about watching them can food for the winter, sew quilts in the summer, run thrift stores, and do everything they could to provide.

And as I spoke, she interrupted me.

She said, "I've heard you talk about them for years—but you've never spoken of them like this."

And she was right.

That moment stayed with me.

I thought: Maybe I've forgiven them—without even realizing it.

Maybe it happened somewhere between writing *Finding Fish*, writing the film *Antwone Fisher*, and speaking to audiences about child abuse.

Somewhere in all those years of remembering and giving voice to the past, forgiveness had found me.

And the way I knew it was:

I didn't feel anger anymore.

Not pity. Not pain.

Just empathy.

And understanding.

Forgiveness didn't arrive like a thunderclap.

It came quietly, over time.

I used to think forgiveness would be something you decide—like snapping your fingers.

But I've come to believe real forgiveness sneaks up on you.

One day you realize you're no longer asking "Why me?"

You're asking,

"What now?"

I don't want to be cruel in return.

I don't want to hurt them—or their children, or grandchildren, or anyone connected to their name.

That's not why I tell the truth.

I tell it because the truth is what freed me.

Back then, I couldn't see anything but the pain.

But now, when I look back, I can see a more complete picture.

I can even see the goodness in them.

And I can say—with a full heart—that I forgive them.

I'm not saying they were right.

I'm saying I forgive them anyway.

Not because I forget. Not because it didn't matter.

But because holding onto anger was too heavy.

Because I know I've needed forgiveness too.

Because we all do.

They're gone now.
But I carry them with me.
And I carry the forgiveness too.
That's what forgiveness gave me—
the freedom to stop asking "Why me?"
and start living in the answer.

My Shyness

People often ask me how I made it through.
How I survived the system. The foster homes. The streets.
How I made good decisions when everything around me suggested otherwise.
    And I usually don't know how to answer that.
Because the truth is, it wasn't always some bold choice I made.
Sometimes, it was just… that I was shy.
    Even as a child, I was quiet. I kept to myself.
I watched more than I spoke.
And when trouble came through the room, I didn't run toward it—I stepped back.
    That might sound small, but in certain environments, that one step back can be the difference between life and death,
between staying free or getting caught up.
My shyness may have looked like weakness, but it protected me.
It made me cautious.
It made me slow to follow. Slow to trust. Slow to act.
And sometimes, that slowness was a blessing.

Then there were the places that kept me isolated: The orphanage.

The reform school.

Even the Navy.

They weren't easy. But they were structured.

Predictable in a way the streets weren't.

In those places, I wasn't pulled into the kind of chaos that swallowed other boys whole.

And I think that structure, combined with my own nature —

my introversion, my sensitivity—formed a kind of quiet shield around me.

I didn't always know it then.

I sometimes hated being shy.

But looking back, I realize it may have saved my life.

There were moments, though—

times when I wanted to belong so badly, or liked the people around me enough to take a risk—

that I stepped out from behind the shield.

I'd speak up more than usual, laugh louder than I felt,

take part in something that didn't feel quite right.

But almost every time, it felt strange.

Like I was outside of myself. Exposed. Off-balance.

As if anything could happen out there.

And so I'd retreat.
Back behind the shield.
Back to where I felt safe.
Back to being me.
Shy.

What Time Doesn't Take

I've always used my imagination to build a world that felt right for me.

Not with me out front, but right in the middle—part of something good.

I found that world in my childhood community of Glenville, in Cleveland.

The friends I made there were the first people I ever chose for myself.

And I've kept them with me all my life.

Some, I still know.
Many have passed on.

But I carried them with me, even when I was away—off in reform school, in the Navy, or just living apart from them.

In my imagination, they stayed frozen in time—exactly how I remembered them when we were young.

The way they laughed.
The corners we stood on.
The classrooms.
The neighborhood.

It never changed in my mind.
It stayed beautiful.

But now, as time passes and more of them are gone, it's like the physical part of that world is slipping away.

Piece by piece.

The Glenville I knew doesn't look the same anymore.

It's been worn down—by time, by poverty, by whatever it is that slowly crumbles a place.

Now I'm left with remnants—just the memories.

But they're still vivid.

Still bright.

My friends are still innocent.

Our lives still unfolding.

Our laughter still echoing in those streets.

Even as I grow older—looking in the mirror and seeing all the changes—I can still return to that world.

And maybe that's the gift.

What time takes from the world,

it can't take from the heart and mind.

From the Outside Looking In

I see a therapist once a week.

We talk about my life—not just the big things or the small ones.

Where I was right.

When I was wrong.

And everything in between.

The things I've accomplished and what I've lost.

What my eyes have seen, and what it taught me.

The things I've survived.

And sometimes, I catch myself—

and step back in surprise.

Because I've done a lot of things I never planned.

Marvelous things.

Not always easy.

Not always joyful.

But remarkable, just the same.

I've traveled the world to places I could never have known existed—breathtaking, frightful, wondrous, mysterious.

Sat with interesting people in strange faraway places I never would've met.

Stood in rooms I never imagined I'd be allowed to enter.

Discovered things about the world—and about myself—

that changed me over and over again.

And still, I remember:

I have dyslexia.

I really struggled with it early on.

But I became a writer.

Not just a writer,

but a New York Times bestselling author whose book was translated into a few languages.

Not just a storyteller and poet,

but a man who wrote a film about his own life—

and watched it be made.

I've written movies for major studios.

Had lunch with the President's family in the private residence of the White House.

Spoken before members of Congress,

and represented the United States overseas on behalf of the U.S. State Department.

I've spoken in theaters,

and held the attention of over two thousand of America's elites in the palms of my hands.

Stood on red carpets, won awards,

sat in boardrooms.

But those aren't even the most extraordinary things.

The real marvel is that I kept going.

That I made something out of so many broken pieces.

There were difficult times.

Really hard times.

Some things I can't even talk about—not yet.

Maybe never.

But I've talked about them in safe places.

And when I look at my life—the whole of it—the joys, the sorrows, the redirections, the recoveries—

it's like a gumbo.

A mix of good and bad,

rich and poor,

up and down,

left turn, right turn, u-turns.

It's not perfect.

But it's full.

And it's mine.

If I wasn't me, looking at this life from the outside,

I think I'd say,

Wow.

Proof of Life

(Reflection Before a Birthday)

My birthday is coming up.

A big one, I feel.

Then again, they're all big now.

I always use this time to check in—physically, emotionally.

I get my checkup.
I take stock.
I look back.

I do that all the time, really.

A lot of my work is the result of looking back.

But something about birthdays brings it into sharper focus.

At this point in my life, it's like watching a movie trailer.

I can see how a lot of it unfolded.

When I was younger, there wasn't much footage.

Now, there's plenty—a long reel of scenes, dialogue, characters.

All kinds of time.

I never really journaled, not in the way people usually mean it.

But I remembered.

And in that way, I suppose I have been journaling all along—just differently.

The key points stayed with me.

Small things.

Even smaller things.

I have a deep memory.

One moment is attached to the next.

That's how I remember.

Music is a bookmark.

Smells are time machines.

Some memories still bring physical feelings.

Even now, I can almost smell a scene from my childhood.

Like the field trip we took in fifth grade to Huff Bakery.

Ms. Brenda Prophit—she was our wonderful teacher.

Huff Bakery—officially Hough Bakery—was a beloved Cleveland staple, founded in 1903 on Hough Avenue in the Hough neighborhood ("Huff"), with dozens of locations and generations of dough and memory.

I can still smell that bakery.

It's faded now—not as strong as it used to be—

but it still gives me that feeling.

Light.

Warm.

Distant.

Sometimes I wonder if remembering is as special to others as it is to me.

I've relied on memory to keep me going.

Not just the good parts—I tried to remember everything.

It reminded me I was still here.

That I'd been through it all.

When I returned to Cleveland once, I tried to gather some childhood friends to celebrate.

One of them kept asking why I was trying to get us all together again.

"You know some of us didn't get along back then," he said.

"I know," I told him.

"I still remember you all as my friends—even the ones I didn't always get along with... like you."

He laughed.

I've thought about that ever since.

Maybe memories mean more to me than they do to others.

Some people don't remember the same music.

The same feeling.

Some childhood friends didn't live long.
They died very, very young.
But I remember them.
And when I do, I feel them in my body.
I remember us all being so young—
so impressionable,
so brand new,
so unaware,
so innocent.

Now, I'm in a time some of those old friends are passing away.
But I'm still here.
Still remembering it all.
I believe life is worth remembering.
Not just yesterday.
Not just the imagined tomorrow.
You've got to go all the way back.
Prove to yourself that you lived.
That you made it.
That it wasn't easy.
That there is joy in life.
And that you're still here.
So yes, my birthday is coming up.
And I feel fortunate to have my memories.
They are my birthday gift to myself.

A treasure I can't afford to lose.
They are my proof of life.
What I have to show for who I am—
on this level of consciousness,
today.

Afterword

One Last Thing Before You Go

I came from the ache of not knowing. What I had were questions—and the dreams. The dreams came first.
Little by little, piece by piece, I found my way. I found my father—years after he was gone. I found the story of my mother—through silence, through stillness, through a single stare across her kitchen. I found the truth and forgiveness for the people who raised me, the people who hurt me, and the ones who'd show me so much love along the way. I found Mercy. I found Valencia. I found Dwight. I found a woman named LaNette, who loved me back. And I became a father to daughters who shine like stars.
But even after all of that—there was something more.
I came to understand that I wasn't just the boy who was abandoned. Or the man who overcame. I was something older.
I was memory passed down through the blood. I was spirit walking through time. I was rooted before I ever knew what a root was. Some things you can't trace with paperwork or photos. Some things live in your whole body and mind.

And that's the biggest thing I've come to believe: I've been here a long time. Not just in this life—but in the great story that came before it. And I wanted to leave this behind, so someone else, somewhere, someday could read it and feel a little less lost. A little more seen. A little more ancient. And a little more known. That's why I reflect. It's why I wrote all this. That's why I had to. If you've made it from Glenville to the deep end, you know now that the water's been the same all along. It wasn't the depth that would have taken you under—only panic could have done that. You didn't panic. You swam to the deep end—you finished this book. You survived.

Acknowledgments

This book would not exist without the grace of others. To the people who showed me kindness, taught me something about life, or believed in me—thank you.

To my wife LaNette, and to my daughters, Azure and Indigo—you've loved me more purely and completely than I could have ever asked for. To be your husband and father has been the greatest joy of my life.

To my friend Todd Black—thank you for helping me find my voice and amplifying it when I couldn't.

To Denzel Washington—thank you for believing in this story and carrying it forward with care and strength.

To Jeff Frankel and Scott Whitehead—in a business that rarely holds on when times are quiet, you never let go.

Special Acknowledgments

Ms. Doris B. James

When I was a child at Oliver Wendell Holmes Elementary School, Ms. James was the principal. To a young boy struggling quietly, she appeared stern and formidable—someone who carried authority without apology. Only later did I come to understand that what I saw as strictness was strength, and care, and a deep sense of responsibility. Years afterward, when I was finally able to read my childhood records, I learned something I had never known: that Ms. James had noticed me. When my truancy came to light, she did more than report it. She expressed concern about my home life and questioned what others seemed willing to overlook. She paid attention when it mattered.

When we reconnected many years later, she remembered me—and she remembered the circumstances. She told me she was proud. That moment reached back across decades and closed a circle I did not know was still open.

Ms. James was a pioneer in her own right—a Black woman leading a school in the early 1960s, carrying authority with dignity. She understood isolation, and she understood compassion. She offered both, quietly, without expectation.

She has since passed on, but I carry her with me. Knowing that someone saw me then—really saw me—has meant more than I can say.

Ms. Brenda Profit

My beloved teacher at Parkwood Elementary for the fourth, fifth, and sixth grades. She created a classroom that felt like home—warm, safe, and full of love. She noticed me, too, and in doing so gave me something priceless: a space where I could learn without fear, where I was seen and cared for. Walking into her classroom was like walking into light.

To Cleveland, Glenville, and every street that shaped me—I carry your lessons and your rhythm with me always.

To my lifelong childhood friends—Michael Shields, Gary Spencer, Pamela Louis, Ulysses Stanton, Sonya Edwards, Donna Edwards, Veloria Edwards, Kenneth Edwards, Jenise Womick, Janine King, and Nathaniel Hayward—the family I chose as a boy.

When I was growing up, I was longing for friends and family. I was quiet. I was shy. I didn't always know how to reach out. But you made it easy. You made space for me. You made me feel welcome. With you, I didn't have to explain myself. I could just be.

You were there in classrooms and on sidewalks, on Parkwood and beyond—laughing, talking, dreaming, surviving. In ways you may never have known, you gave me something I needed more than anything at that time: belonging.

We are still connected. We still talk. We still remember. And that tells me everything about what we meant to each other.

Thank you for choosing me, too—when I needed it most. And to the reader: thank you for sitting with these memories. Thank you for listening.

About the Author

Antwone Fisher is a writer whose work explores memory, identity, and the long arc of healing. Raised in foster care, he has spent his life giving language to experiences often left unspoken—stories shaped by endurance, reflection, and the search for belonging.

His writing is grounded in lived experience and guided by a belief in the power of truth told plainly. Across memoir, film, and now reflection, Fisher returns again and again to the idea that survival is not only about what we endure, but what we learn to carry with care.

Reflections Beneath the Buckeye Trees is his most personal work to date—a gathering of moments, lessons, and quiet reckonings drawn from a life lived attentively.

Also by Antwone Fisher

Finding Fish: a memoir

Who Will Cry For The Little Boy

A Boy Should Know How To Tie A Tie
And Other Lessons For Succeeding In Life

www.ingramcontent.com/pod-product-compliance
Lightning Source LLC
Chambersburg PA
CBHW020250070526
44119CB00138B/460/J